PENGUIN BOOKS

GETTING THINGS DONE FOR TEENS

David Allen is an internationally best-selling author who is widely recognized as the world's leading expert on personal and organizational productivity. *Time* magazine called his flagship book, *Getting Things Done,* "the definitive business self-help book of the decade."

Mike Williams was president and CEO of the David Allen Company from 2011 to 2016, is on the board of directors for the Association for Talent Development (td.org), and is the Getting Things Done Enterprise Architect at Zappos .com

Mark Wallace has taught in public schools in Minnesota for more than twenty years and has won the TIES Distinguished Educator Award.

Getting Things Done

for Teens

Take Control of Your Life in a Distracting World

David Allen,

Mike Williams, and Mark Wallace

PENGUIN BOOKS

PENGUIN BOOKS
An imprint of Penguin Random House LLC
375 Hudson Street
New York, New York 10014
penguin.com

LIBRARY OF CONGRESS CATALOGING-IN-PUBLICATION DATA
Names: Allen, David, 1945 December 28– author.
Title: Getting things done : take control of your life in a distracting world
    / David Allen, Mike Williams, and Mark Wallace.
Description: New York : Penguin Books, [2018] | Includes index.
Identifiers: LCCN 2018013261 (print) | LCCN 2018013684 (ebook) |
    ISBN 9780525503729 (e-book) | ISBN 9780143131939 (pbk.)
Subjects: LCSH: Time management—Juvenile literature. |
    Self-management (Psychology)—Juvenile literature. |
    Distraction (Psychology)—Juvenile literature.
Classification: LCC BF637.T5 (ebook) | LCC BF637.T5 A453 2018 (print) |
    DDC 646.7—dc23
LC record available at https://lccn.loc.gov/2018013261

ISBN 9780143131939 (pbk.)
ISBN 9780525503729 (ebook)

Printed in the United States of America
10 9 8 7 6 5 4 3 2 1

Set in Mercury Text G1 with DIN Next LT Pro
Designed by Daniel Lagin

David Allen

For a new generation of young people, who will see problems as projects sooner than we did.

Mike Williams

For Arianna, Hannah, and Conrad, you inspire me, encourage me, and teach me. For caring adults everywhere looking to make a difference.

Mark Wallace

For my amazing wife, wonderful children, selfless family, supportive friends, and everyone who has the courage to take the single next action.

Contents

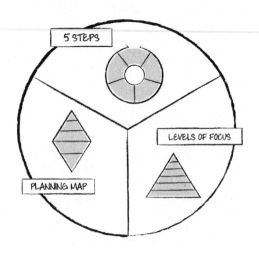

Part 2: The Practice of GTD 49

Part 3: The Lab 191

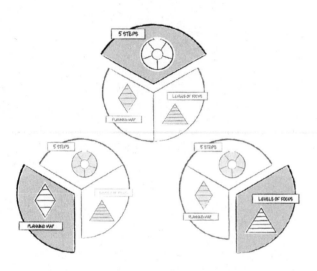

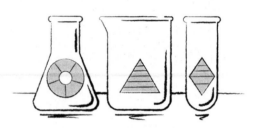

For Additional Information

Visit gtdforteens.com for additional information, stories, and resources.

Follow gtdforteens on Twitter, Instagram, Snapchat, Pinterest, Facebook, and YouTube.

Tag us with #gtdforteens.

Acknowledgments

We'd like to thank the countless parents, teachers, counselors, and clergy who, after experiencing the GTD methodology, have pleaded for something for "our kids," wishing they had had it for themselves in their formative years. This has been a key factor in our motivation to craft *Getting Things Done for Teens*.

Mark and Mike would like to thank David Allen for inviting us to work on this project. Beyond inspiring us through the original *Getting Things Done*, your wisdom, guidance, sense of humor, love, and generosity are humbling and inspiring.

We would like to thank Joe Beard and his team at Bionic Giant (bionicgiant.com) for their guidance and support on the illustrations as well as, most important, their desire to encourage this effort to improve the lives of teens around the world.

We'd like to thank Meg Edwards for her effort and support in the early days of this project. Her passion for helping kids and adults is eternal and inspiring. Specifically, her mastery of applying her knowledge of ADD and ADHD with GTD is innovative and has brought relief and joy to many adults and students. She is one of the best in the industry in this area. Thank you for sharing your passion, wisdom, and expertise.

There are so many people who gave of their time and wisdom to help the evolution of this book. We'd like to thank Monica Russell, Lizzie Chapin, Ana Armstrong, and Hannah Williams for their editorial suggestions. We'd like to thank Doe Coover for guiding us from the earliest stages of this project. Many thanks to Rick Kot and the team at Penguin for helping us get the book across the finish line and into the hands of teens and caring adults worldwide.

There is a whole host of people who touched this project and to whom we send our gratitude, and apologies to those many unnamed individuals who helped along the way (you know who you are). Special thanks to Annie Gott, Conrad Williams, Todd Wallace, Louis and Maxim Kim, Jeff Boliba, Deb Pekarek, Charles Fred, Tristan Zarate, Peter Hodne, Rooms 7&8, Maggie Weiss, Frank Sopper, the Mack family, Dan Roam, Jeff Irby, Amanda Doyle, Evan Taubenfeld, Kyle Steel, Krissee Chasseur, Jason Spafford, and Kevin Brune.

Foreword

"Boy, I wish I had learned this in school—it would have made such a difference!"

"How can I get this to my kids?!"

I've heard innumerable such exclamations over the past three decades, as I've trained and coached people in the methodology now known around the world as "GTD," described in my flagship book, *Getting Things Done.*

For those of you familiar with GTD, these sentiments probably resonate with you. If you are not aware of the method, this book will give you a great taster of the kinds of practices that we all should have learned in our early years but didn't. It's a simple but profound way to deal with the things that have our attention, so that we become the masters of them instead of their victims.

The desire for a method to deliver these practices to younger people, and as soon as possible, has been expressed to me often by parents, teachers, school administrators, clergy, and counselors—people with caring roles in helping young people prepare themselves for their lives ahead.

I am not a parent, nor am I a teacher in the traditional education system. What I developed over these many years was a model of best practices that became the core of my profession, providing training and coaching, primarily in the corporate world. This was the population that was at the forefront of the bombardment of email, the internet, and the ever-increasing disruptions of rapid change in that world, and they were hungry for help.

I knew from the beginning what I had uncovered was extremely useful for anyone with a creative and busy life, ranging from students and artists to stay-at-home parents. What I didn't know was how to reach that audience effectively, as I was trying to build my own career. And I certainly didn't know the best way to translate the methodology into an understandable and usable format for teenagers.

That said, I always had the sense that if my work was to have the long-term impact I thought it could, kids would be the answer. In order to have a sustainable experience of stress-free productivity, there are behavioral habits that most adults find challenging to change—for instance, keeping track of every commitment, large and small, in a trusted external system instead of in their heads. This simple but powerful practice creates the ability to think optimally and focus creatively. Most adults won't do this, even when they know better. I've seen it. Kids can get this quickly. I've seen it.

Most adults think they know how to think. Kids are at a place where they can begin to learn.

How (and if) I could reach that younger audience was unknown to me, though it always remained on my "Someday/Maybe" list. My own wishful thinking in this regard started to morph into a real possibility with the emergence of two people in my world: Mike Williams and Mark Wallace.

I met Mike when I heard about his work at General Electric, successfully applying my methods in his role managing significant change there. I then discovered he had been blogging about his exploration in translating the GTD method, with success, for his own kids! We stayed in touch, and Mike eventually came on board with me professionally in our company. (People on my staff who had met him said, "I want Mike as my dad!") We agreed that it might be time to at last write this book, and I knew he was the guy who could do the heavy lifting for that.

Then I heard about a man named Mark Wallace, an elementary school teacher in Minneapolis who had become such a fan of GTD that he had begun to incorporate its principles and techniques with the kids in his school. I had the opportunity to visit his classroom, where I saw the students doing a core practice of stress-free productivity—what we call the Weekly Review. It's what people who know my methods realize is the key behavior to make GTD stick, but few do it with any consistency. In Mark's class, all thirty kids were totally engaged in it, and they were all younger than twelve years old! Obviously Mark had to be on our team.

Mike and Mark will tell their own stories here. They have certainly added credibility beyond my scope in their engagement with the younger set. And they added and applied their expertise for us to create a wonderful educational experience for anyone willing to get involved with GTD—young and old.

This book is the "simplicity beyond complexity" ideal that Oliver Wendell Holmes extolled. If you're ready, use it to turbocharge your life in a really cool way. If you think you're beyond any of this, don't kid yourself.

—David Allen

Introduction to Parents, Teachers, and Other Caring Adults

Welcome! If you are reading this book, you are probably a caring adult (e.g., a parent, teacher, family member, friend, clergy, or mentor) who wants to support a teen in your world.

What have you noticed about these young people?

- Is their distraction, stress, or worry increasing or decreasing?
- Have you noticed what has their attention?
- Have you noticed things concerning them (e.g., what's taking place in the school lunchroom, on the bus, on social media apps), things they are on their own to figure out?
- Have you noticed a budding talent or passion that just needs a little direction or focus?

Today, you may be the guiding hand helping your teen navigate school and life. In a few short years, they will need to have the foundation to handle the freedom, rising complexity, and free-form nature of life on their own. Wouldn't it be gratifying if you could teach them the techniques and habits for navigating life, much like you taught them how to ride a bike, play a sport or musical instrument, or learn to drive?

Good news! We designed this book to serve as a resource to help teens build proficiency in the foundational skills for navigating life. These skills will help them reduce distraction, a sense of being overwhelmed, and stress while increasing their self-confidence, presence, productivity, creativity, and fun.

The Getting Things Done (GTD) methodology is practiced worldwide. The first generation of practitioners were adults (e.g., artists, executives, business owners, scientists, doctors, teachers, clergy, moms, dads, and many more) who learned to replace less effective habits with more effective ones. A common response to learning GTD has been, "I wish I would have learned this in school!" We've written this as the textbook for that missing life-skill class.

Before you start your journey with the teen (or teens) in your life, let's go back in time for a moment. Do you remember the first time . . .

- You worked on your first significant school project?
- You had to track your own homework and deadlines?
- You tried out for a team or an activity?
- You took driving lessons?
- You got your first taste of freedom when you left home—perhaps for college or to live on your own?

How'd those first-time experiences go? If you're like most people, they were a little rough. Yet, over time, as you accumulated life experience, many of them got much easier.

As you work through this book with your teens, they will undoubtedly experience—and work through—many of their own "firsts." As a caring adult, you will probably feel the short-term tug of "let me jump in and fix it" versus the long-term wisdom of "I need to have patience and let them figure it out for themselves." This book will help you handle the short-term needs and, using the Getting Things Done methodology, teach your teens the tools and behaviors that will help them in the long term.

You can think of this book as a tool kit that contains foundational principles and processes that can last a lifetime. They are simple. They are teachable. They are timeless.

If you are unfamiliar with the Getting Things Done method, we suggest you take a moment to flip through this book. You may find that working through the book alongside your teen has the added benefit of helping you.

We hope this book serves you and your teen as a trusted source of practical wisdom as you enter, traverse, and exit the formative teenage years. It is our hope that as the teens in your world exit their teen years, they have the know-how to follow their dreams and handle whatever life throws their way. Bon voyage.

Introduction to Teenagers

Welcome! Somehow you found this book (or the book found you).

If you do nothing else, take just a few seconds to take a quick look through it from front to back. This is not an ordinary book. It's both a guidebook and a tool kit for life—your life.

You are moving through some interesting times and dealing with lots of stuff. Your parents or teachers may know some of what is going on in your world, but only you know all of it. You're juggling classes, sports, activities, family, friendships, and more. You live in a hyperconnected world. One day you could be having a great day, and then suddenly, a *ding* or comment or photo on your phone or computer changes everything. It could be something exciting or disturbing, but in either case, it's something that has your attention, and something you need to somehow deal with in addition to everything else you already have to do. How do you manage it all?

This book will help you by giving you the wisdom and tools you need to find the answer. It will help decrease your stress and worry. It will help increase your ability to handle things so you have more time to hang out with your friends or simply relax and do nothing.

You can explore this book by yourself, or you may want to journey through it with a friend, mentor, or parent. Test the ideas. Discover what works for you today. Build on that. As your world grows more complex, read through the book again, as it's full of ideas that can help you through all the grades and stages of your life.

Enjoy the adventure.

Before We Begin

READY?

"Are you ready for middle school?"

"Are you ready for high school?"

"Are you ready for college?"

"Are you ready for your test?"

"Are you ready for your presentation?"

"Are you ready to go?"

Do these questions sound familiar? Some are larger life questions; others are smaller. What they have in common is *change*.

There is nothing simple about being you. It may seem as if you're always facing new challenges and transitions and getting asked the question "Are you ready?" How do you answer?

Take a few seconds and think about your life today and what's coming your way in the near future and *really* ask yourself: Are you . . . **ready**? Even if you don't have a full answer to this question yet, that's okay! This book is here to help you answer this question with a deeper confidence.

USING THIS GUIDEBOOK

Welcome to *Getting Things Done for Teens*, a tool kit full of principles, practices, and tips for you to apply to whatever comes your way. We've designed it with you, the individual, in mind. Because no two people are alike, and because everyone has different learning styles and preferences, we've designed this book to be read and used in several different ways.

You'll find that it's visual and interactive.

In it you will find a full cast of memorable characters along with a variety of maps that will help define the territory. The characters help represent concepts, while the maps will give these concepts a working form. Some of the maps will help you practice new ways of thinking, and others will help you capture your thoughts and organize your own thinking.

We've also created a series of activities for you to test out and see which principles work best for you. The examples were inspired by real people, and we'd like to hear how *you* apply the principles in your world.

HOW THE BOOK IS ORGANIZED

Part 1 will take a look at everyday life and what's happening in the world around you. What new and exciting opportunities are out there? What pitfalls are waiting to trip you up?

Part 2 will introduce you to the principles, practices, and tools you can use to succeed in your everyday life. These will help you build habits toward experiencing what we call the "ready state."

Part 3 will give you the opportunity to put these principles, practices, and tools to the test. Here you will get to play, experiment, and practice so you can discover what works for you.

Now that we've introduced you to the three main parts of the book, let's explain what we mean by **ready**.

WHAT IS READY?

adjective (**readier, readiest**)

1 [predic.] in a suitable state for an activity, action, or situation; fully prepared

verb (**readies, readying, readied**) [with obj.]

prepare (someone or something) for an activity or purpose

There are many official definitions for the word "ready," but what does it really mean? What do you think of when you hear "**ready**"? Do you hear your mother asking, "Are you ready yet?" Do you hear the sound of a referee's whistle starting the game? Do you picture the curtain opening for a performance? Do you hear your teacher saying, "Are you ready? You can now begin the test."

Being ready can have different meanings, but in this book, we're going to define "ready" as a combination of four things:

1. READY for now
2. READY for what's next
3. READY for transitions
4. READY for anything

Let's take a look at each.

Are You Ready for Now?

Ready for now means being present, right now, in the current moment.

What kind of ready is this? It's your ability to stay fully focused on one thing—like reading this sentence.

Some examples of being ready for now:

- Are you ready to read this book?
- Are you ready to practice your instrument?
- Are you ready to hang out with friends?
- Are you ready to ask someone out?
- Are you ready to start your homework?
- Are you ready to listen to a friend who needs to talk to you?

Are You Ready for What's Next?

Ready for what's next means being fully aware of things that need to be done over a given period of time.

What kind of ready is this? It's an intuition that comes with understanding what you need to do and a feeling of confidence about how and when you will do it.

Some examples of being ready for what's next:

- Are you ready for math class next period?
- Are you ready for soccer practice today?
- Are you ready for your job interview?
- Are you ready for your trip this weekend?

Are You Ready for Transitions?

Being ready for transitions means having the ability to handle shifts in key areas of your life.

What kind of ready is this? It's your ability to react and respond effectively to change. You will experience significant shifts in responsibilities from middle school through high school graduation. These will be exciting and dynamic years, and it's actually possible to be prepared and feel ready for these shifts.

Some examples of being ready for transitions:

- Are you ready to transition from middle school to high school?
- Are you ready to transition from high school to college?
- Are you ready to transition from noncompetitive to competitive sports?
- Are you ready to transition from not having a job to having a job after school?
- Are you ready to transition from high school to working full-time?
- Are you ready to transition from living at home to living on your own?

Are You Ready for Anything?

Ready for anything means being relaxed and ready for whatever comes your way.

What kind of ready is this? It's the feeling that comes from knowing how to gain control and perspective. A big part of *being* ready is *feeling* ready. It's a mind-set of anticipation and confidence in knowing you have what it takes to live your life to its fullest, take risks, and find success.

Some examples of being ready for anything:

- Are you ready to try something new?
- Are you ready to take on something that is really challenging and may result in failure?
- Are you ready to tackle a dream you have?
- Are you ready for that important conversation with _____?
- Are you ready to move from home to college?

This book is here to help equip you to feel ready and confident in any type of situation you face. So with that in mind . . . are you ready to begin?

To maximize this learning, it's helpful to have a basic understanding of what's going on inside your head from day to day, minute to minute, moment to moment. Your brain is the most powerful and complicated tool you possess, so let's start by describing a few of its capacities and limitations and the signals it sends. (This section is not meant to be a thorough presentation on brain research. If you find yourself interested in going deeper, we'd recommend *The Organized Mind* by Daniel J. Levitin or *BrainChains* by Theo Compernolle.)

YOUR BRAIN

We're going to focus here on just two areas of the brain, one of which is responsible for quick reactions and the other for deeper thinking and decision-making. These two areas will be critical in understanding and applying the principles in this book. To help you understand how they function, we've created two characters to illustrate each of them.

Meet Myggy and Cortland

The first important part of the brain for our purposes is called the **amygdala**.

The amygdala is your brain's front line of defense for fight or flight. It serves as a scan-and-response system for everything that enters your world. It is on autopilot, always searching for new inputs. If the amygdala senses danger or a threat, it will alert your body, activating it in the form of fear, adrenaline, stress, anxiety, sleeplessness, or other stressors. The amygdala kicks your body into a higher gear and will continue alerting you until whatever is troubling it gets taken care of.

If a car is coming, it will prompt you to jump out of the way. If a baseball is hit right at you, it will help you react and make a spectacular catch. It can provide you with a boost of adrenaline if you need to step in and help a friend in danger. Your amygdala is meant to work fast and in short bursts on an as-needed basis.

The continual alerts issued by the amygdala can make you feel a lot like you have a monkey jabbering and freaking out inside your head. This aspect of the brain is sometimes referred to as the "monkey brain." In this book, we'll use the character of Myggy the monkey as the symbol for the amygdala at work.

AMYGDALA

SELF
INVOLVED

NO SENSE OF
TIME, ONLY THE
PRESENT MOMENT

EXTREMELY
FAST MOVING

RANDOM TASK
SWITCHER

HIGHLY
REACTIVE

MYGGY
The Amygdala Monkey

The second important part of the brain is called the prefrontal cortex, located on the frontal lobe.

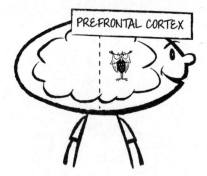

The prefrontal cortex is the part of the brain whose function is analytical thought and decision-making. It is responsible for problem solving and synthesizes and makes meaning from all that you see and do.

The prefrontal cortex is key to learning, creating, imagining, building and developing relationships, and making things happen. In contrast to the amygdala, the prefrontal cortex is *not* on autopilot. You engage the prefrontal cortex when you slow down and *think*, as well as when your mind is idle and has time to wander. The prefrontal cortex requires some time, space, and energy to function efficiently, and it can be trained to be even more effective.

The prefrontal cortex is like a wise old owl watching over the forest of your life—calmly and slowly observing, thinking, and developing a deep and experienced wisdom to make sense of life's experiences. We'll use the character of Cortland the owl as the symbol of the prefrontal cortex.

WISE AND
EMPATHIC

SLOW,
DELIBERATE

ANALYTICAL AND
SEQUENTIAL

LIMITLESS
CAPABILITIES,
IMAGINATIVE,
CREATIVE

PROACTIVE

CORTLAND
The Prefrontal Cortex Wise Owl

To be ready in all the ways we have described, you'll need to understand and harness the powers of both of these parts of your brain. Myggy talks and sends signals; Cortland listens and responds.

When this relationship is in sync, being **ready** is possible. When it is out of sync, some unhealthy and unproductive habits can form.

So, how do you become ready? What do you need to do? What's in it for you? What keeps you from just doing this naturally? What impact does this all have on you? Why should you care?

Stay tuned. We are just getting started.

Rule your mind, or it will rule you.   —HORACE

Part 1
The Art of Getting Things Done

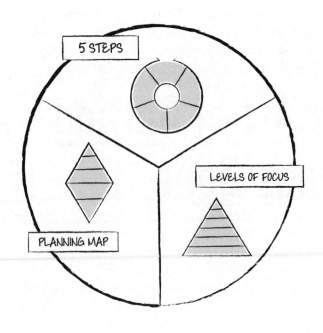

THE GETTING THINGS DONE (GTD) METHODOLOGY

GTD is an acronym for Getting Things Done—a way of thinking that helps people gain better control and focus in their lives, no matter what they are doing. GTD is not *really* about getting things "done." It's about learning to become focused on and engaged with the present, being aware of what is next, finding stability when things feel out of control, and creatively anticipating whatever life has to offer, whether that involves school, work, relationships, sports, goals, dreams, or even video games. GTD is about being **ready** for it all.

We have seen people from all over the world benefit from the practice of GTD, ranging in ages from eight to eighty, plus or minus a few years on both ends of that spectrum. GTD can be used by anyone, of any background, any gender, any religion, any culture, at any time, in any situation. It is an approach that, once learned, can be developed, personalized, and used for the rest of your life. Much like music, dance, and sports, it is an art that involves learning, practicing, and integrating into your life.

GTD has three main parts:

1. **Five Steps**—to help you gain control
2. **Levels of Focus**—to help you gain perspective
3. A **Planning Map**—to help you gain both control and perspective for situations and projects that require deeper thinking

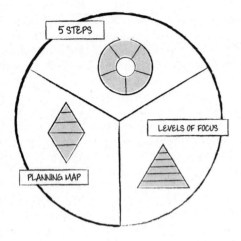

Explore each of these tools and strategies and decide what works best for you. Once you put the GTD way of thinking to the test, you'll find that it will help you succeed, and you'll *want* to learn more about how you can make these tools and strategies your own.

Some questions that might be preoccupying you:

"Why should I learn this?"

"Why have I not heard of this before from my parents or teachers?"

"Is this going to create more work for me?"

"Why can't I just do what I've always done, if it's worked for me so far?"

"What _____?"

"Why _____?"

These are all natural and good concerns, but let's look at *why* a new mind-set and skill set might be needed for your unique generation.

THE PROBLEM

Rising Complexity

Have you noticed how complicated the world is becoming? Have you noticed how complicated *your* world is becoming?

For example, can you remember a time, not so long ago, when you *thought* that you had a lot of homework? It probably seems laughable in comparison to the amount of homework you have now. What else in your life can you look back on that seems so much simpler, easier, or more straightforward compared to your life today?

Or, do you ever find yourself looking ahead and wishing you could fast-forward a bit to the next stage of your life? For example, do you wish you could have the freedom that comes with having a driver's license and a car? Or do you wish you could just hurry up and move on from middle school into high school, or from high school into college?

Do you notice anything here? Perhaps a pattern?

Life seems to find a way to get a bit more complicated every year. As this is happening, you also continue to change, grow, and respond to these added layers of complexity. Sometimes the complexity matches your ability to handle it quite well. Other times, it doesn't.

When complexities arrive at perfect times in your life, you are challenged in welcoming and exciting directions. You might experience the thrill of new levels of independence, new types of relationships, new learning, and new levels of competition. When this ideal timing happens, you might feel a positive sense of balance and growth. When have *you* felt this way? When was the last change in complexity that came just at the right time?

Sometimes, though, complexity comes *faster* than you are ready to handle. At these times, you might feel stressed and anxious, because there may be *more* change or *more* things to track than you currently know how to deal with or more homework or more activities or more work to manage than you feel capable of handling. Have you ever felt like this? How did you respond?

There are even times where you are desperate for *new* complexity—in any form. You might feel uninspired, even bored, in your current circumstances, and believe that you're more than ready for *more*. You may be hungry for a challenge.

At these times, you might experience a sense of unease until something changes, until there is something novel to explore—a new class, a new hobby, a new relationship, etc.

Have you ever felt that your current situations are stalled and that you're waiting for something unexpected, different, more, or bigger? How did you deal with it?

Managing the complexities of life is a dynamic process. Life continues to evolve, change, and shift—and so do you—sometimes at a comfortable rate, sometimes at an uncomfortable rate.

As you start the journey into this book, ask yourself, "How do I feel about the complexity of my life *today*?" Are you feeling overextended? Perhaps stressed? Underchallenged? Maybe you're currently bored out of your mind? Maybe you're stretched to the point of breaking in some areas of your life and bored in others.

Using the following complexity graph, place an "X" in the spot that best describes you today.

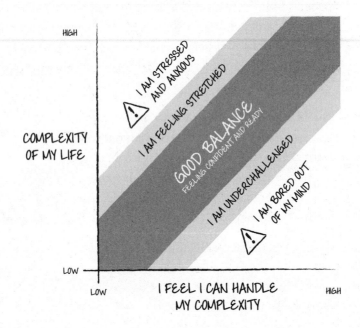

Most likely there have been points in your life when you've experienced some form of all these feelings. Whatever you think of the balance of *today*, the reality is that changes are coming and will continue to come. These shifts in complexity and the feelings that go with them are natural. Eventually, you will graduate high school and go on to college or get a job. You will decide where you will live, how you'll support yourself, and what kind of impact you want to make. You may decide to get married and raise a family. With each of these transitions, your life will become more complex, and that complexity will require new responses from you.

While everyone, including your parents and teachers, has experienced these shifts as they've made their way through life, *your* experience will be different, and it is important that you understand why.

The better you get, the better you better get.   —DAVID ALLEN

Connectivity and the Flood of Information

While it is true that every generation faces a world that is unlike the generation before it, your situation is different, because the world you're facing is *vastly* different. What worked in the past may not work for you, because something new appeared that has changed everything.

Do you know what it is? Massive digital connectivity. *Massive.*

We humans are more connected than we have ever been before. Our constant connectivity has transformed how we study, work, play, shop, travel, relate, and communicate. It has also transformed our brains themselves and even how we think.

Many young people are so immersed in this connectivity that they're not even aware of it. Many carry their phones at all times and sleep with them at their bedside. Beeps, vibrations, and notifications all constantly compete for attention—so much so that many

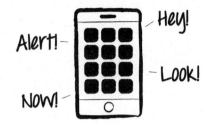

actually feel their phone vibrate when it isn't moving at all. The apps on phones are masterfully designed to grab and hold attention. (How long is your Snapchat streak? How many Instagram followers do you have? How many likes on your picture?) How many times do you check your phone in any given hour?

When you put down your phone, how long can you go before you feel the need to pick it up again? During the time you've spent reading this book, have you been tempted to check your phone or mobile device for new information? Did your phone *interrupt* you?

Try this: Take out your device. Shut it off—don't just put it to sleep; shut it down completely. Now pause for a few minutes. What do you notice? How do you feel?

If you're in a public place while reading this, stop and take a look around. What do you see? The answer will be clear: We all look like chipmunks, but instead of holding nuts, we are holding phones.

Our digital habits, like any other habit, are affecting our brains and nervous systems. Bits of information are coming in faster and in larger numbers than ever before. The reactive part of the brain is highly stimulated, and in extreme cases, it is overstimulated to such a degree that it may actually be forming an addiction to digital stimulation. The amygdala is designed to deal with short-term bursts of stimuli, not to be in a constant state of high alert.

Yours will be the first generation to grow up in a world where people are connected—to one another, to other cultures, to other countries—*all* the time. That puts you in uncharted territory. You have freedoms and advantages that no previous generation has ever dreamed of. The world's knowledge is at your fingertips, and you have more opportunities than anyone else in the history of the world.

Given that power, what does the next decade, *your* adult future, have in store?

What Will You Need to Succeed?

The truth is that no one knows exactly where we're all headed. No one knows or can predict the exact knowledge or skills you'll need to succeed in this new and hyperconnected world.

Your parents, teachers, and mentors are doing their best to help you be ready to face it. Your school is trying to prepare you, but the truth is that many of the jobs it is getting you ready for don't exist yet and haven't even been imagined or invented. Schools around the world are working hard to modernize and change the way they teach, but their efforts are often far too slow.

Because this is all so unprecedented, you will be in many respects on your own and have to start preparing yourself for this future. There is, however, one human skill that we're certain will be more valuable than ever before and can never be automated. That skill is the ability to *think*—to conceive of new ideas and make them happen.

Thinking is the critical skill that will always be in demand. It will help you in the present moment as well as define what you to do next. In a few years it will help you find a job. It will help you handle situations in which there are no clear answers, directions, or instructions. It will enable you to confront whatever challenges life throws your way.

But there's a problem: This critical aptitude to think is in real danger.

If you find yourself in a hole, stop digging.　　　　—WILL ROGERS

Thinking?

The ability to think—to deeply, imaginatively, and creatively think—is being threatened by the huge amounts of information supplied by connectivity, amounts that have never been

seen before. Inputs are coming at all of us in many novel forms and through many new channels. All of this stuff can burden, disrupt, or even eliminate actual thinking.

You were born into a world where this level of stimulation feels normal, and you may actually think you're used to it. The reality, though, is that you also may have developed some unhealthy habits—or even no habits at all—in learning to deal with it all. Without even knowing it, your habits may be hurting your ability to effectively deal with your everyday life and your ability to think. In fact, many young people have been reporting higher levels of stress and anxiety than we've ever seen.

The data in the following graph is from the American Psychological Association, which conducted research with teenagers in which they measure how much stress they were experiencing.

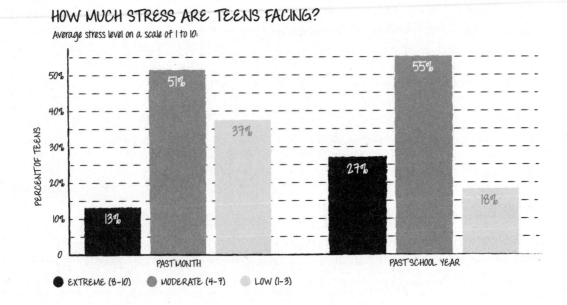

HOW MUCH STRESS ARE TEENS FACING?

Average stress level on a scale of 1 to 10:

- ● EXTREME (8-10)
- ● MODERATE (4-7)
- ● LOW (1-3)

According to this study, about two-thirds of students are living with moderate to extreme amounts of stress. You don't have to be a statistician to know that's a lot.

In addition to the sheer amount of stuff entering their world every day, young people are facing more and more pressure to perform well, test successfully, get into college, find a job, have relationships, hold relationships, feel accepted, make time for friends, get fit, stay fit, and manage sports/music/extracurricular activities . . . and they are expected to deal with more and more of this pressure on their own. Many have calendars that are booked from morning to night, with no free time.

The specific sources of stress for teenagers are diverse.

What areas feel true to you?

WHAT ARE THE SOURCES OF STRESS FOR TEENS?

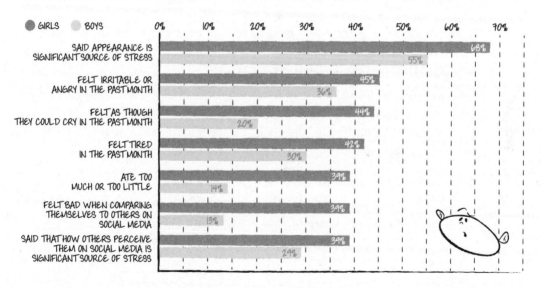

GIRLS ● BOYS ●

SAID APPEARANCE IS SIGNIFICANT SOURCE OF STRESS	Girls: 68% / Boys: 55%
FELT IRRITABLE OR ANGRY IN THE PAST MONTH	Girls: 45% / Boys: 36%
FELT AS THOUGH THEY COULD CRY IN THE PAST MONTH	Girls: 44% / Boys: 20%
FELT TIRED IN THE PAST MONTH	Girls: 42% / Boys: 30%
ATE TOO MUCH OR TOO LITTLE	Girls: 39% / Boys: 14%
FELT BAD WHEN COMPARING THEMSELVES TO OTHERS ON SOCIAL MEDIA	Girls: 39% / Boys: 13%
SAID THAT HOW OTHERS PERCEIVE THEM ON SOCIAL MEDIA IS SIGNIFICANT SOURCE OF STRESS	Girls: 39% / Boys: 29%

These stressful situations decrease opportunities to think. Your ability to think—to conceive of ideas and make them happen—requires thinking *space*. If you know how to create high-quality space for thinking, you will be able to get more done, with less energy and less time.

You are absolutely a pioneer in a new world. As you explore, you'll likely need new tools, new skills, and a new way of thinking to navigate it. Before we introduce you to this novel way of thinking, let's identify some of the pitfalls that could trip you up.

> We cannot solve our problems with the same thinking we used when we created them.
> —Albert Einstein

PITFALLS

A pitfall is a hidden or not easily recognized danger or difficulty.

PITFALL

If you think of being ready as the goal of a game, pitfalls may be placed in the course of it to try to make things difficult or dangerous for you. The same is true in life: Pitfalls are waiting to "catch" you. There are many pitfalls in today's reality that can trip you up, and it's possible you haven't been paying much attention to them. For example, have you ever pulled out your phone or device, intending to quickly check just one thing, and then you see a notification on another app and find yourself still on the device twenty minutes later?

Giving a name, or label, to some common **pitfalls** can help you recognize, acknowledge, and manage them as they appear. There are two main pitfalls that impact a lot of us today, creeping into our lives in sneaky ways.

Pitfall 1: Overload and Overwhelm

Overload: A load with too great a burden

Overwhelm: To overpower in thought or feeling

It's not unusual to feel as if everything coming at you is all just too much, too complicated, too fast, and too frequent. This sensation of there simply being "too much" is an indicator of the pitfall called **overload**.

Overload can sneak up on you. One day you feel in good balance, but two days later a perfect storm hits at school. All your teachers give you homework on the same day you already have a busy after-school activity schedule. If it is not properly handled, this experience of overload will lead to an increased feeling of **overwhelm** and stress.

The growth of overload and overwhelm has a variety of sources. School has recently changed a lot, as it no longer refers only to a building or is confined to textbooks. Classes, projects, and homework continue in the digital world long after you leave your campus. Schoolwork and responsibilities can occupy you all day long.

You don't leave your friends behind after school, either. You can see what they're doing, know what they're talking about, and connect with everyone you know 24/7. Trying to manage and keep up with this stream of constant information can feel like trying to drink from a firehose.

AM I OVERLOADED?

So what exactly does overload look and feel like? How do *you* know if *you* are experiencing it?

Overload can be experienced differently by different people:

> "I can't fall asleep. My mind won't shut down."
>
> "I keep forgetting to _____."
>
> "I feel like I have so much to keep track of."
>
> "I know I should be doing _____, but I _____."
>
> "I have a lot to do, and I just don't know where to begin."
>
> "I can't find what I need when I need it, and it stresses me out."
>
> "I sometimes feel anxious and overwhelmed."
>
> "I can't keep up with everything."

What can you do if you recognize these signs of overload? The tools and strategies in this book can help.

You don't need more genius.
You need less resistance.

—Seth Godin

Pitfall 2: Distraction

"Pay attention!"

"Focus!"

Have you ever heard these warnings from a parent or a teacher?

In the twenty-first century, where information and connectivity are everywhere, the ability to focus attention is being challenged in more ways than ever before. You'll need to protect this ability from constant **distraction**.

Ask yourself this question: When you have a free moment in your day, what do you normally do? Where do you place your focus?

There is a popular myth that humans are good at multitasking—doing more than one thing at a time. While it's true that you may be *capable* of listening to music while texting while watching YouTube while hanging with friends while updating social media, you do this all at a cost . . . the cost of your attention. If your ability to focus gets you results, it would make sense that you should be wary of things that *decrease* that ability.

Distraction is powerful, and, if you're not careful, it can consume hours, days, weeks, months, even years of your life. One of the most common times that we experience distraction is when we're stressed, as it's a quick way to escape these stressful feelings. Distraction can provide a numbing effect on reality, at least temporarily.

Take a look at these statistics regarding stress:

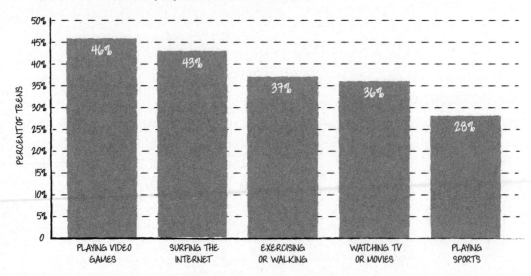

HOW DO TEENS MANAGE THEIR STRESS?

(Bar chart — PERCENT OF TEENS on vertical axis from 0 to 50%)

- PLAYING VIDEO GAMES: 46%
- SURFING THE INTERNET: 43%
- EXERCISING OR WALKING: 37%
- WATCHING TV OR MOVIES: 36%
- PLAYING SPORTS: 28%

What role do you think distraction plays in each of them? Does your own coping strategy work for you, or might it actually be a pitfall?

When else might you be distracted? What might the sources of distraction be? What role is your phone or device playing?

Remember that the amygdala is highly attuned to distraction.

It was designed to scan and react to a more primitive world, and it enabled our early ancestors to notice subtle movements, such as moving twigs and branches, because behind that movement, dinner might be lurking—or something that wanted *them* for dinner! In our modern world, the equivalent of twitching twigs is the digital jungle on phones and computers.

If you choose to surrender to distraction over the things you genuinely value and find most important, then those things that you value won't get your attention or the best of your qualities. Instead, you become *reactive*, which in turn can lead to becoming self-involved. It can lead you into becoming a fast-moving, random task switcher, and distraction wins.

However, if you direct your focus on the things that are truly important to you, then *you* win. You avoid the pitfall of distraction and can then think, create, imagine, and get beyond yourself and now.

GTD can help you focus on the things that are most important to you.

We Are All Alone in This Together

These pitfalls, feelings, and experiences are not unique to you. If you have experienced any one of them, *you are normal*. Everyone, whether young or old, is working through these amazing new opportunities and challenging pitfalls.

This book will offer tools to help you avoid these pitfalls. It will not only enable you to recognize them, name them, and understand the possible effects of not dealing with them, but it will also help you manage your attention and thrive. To do so, we will show you how to reach and maintain what we call the **ready state**.

> If everything was perfect, you would never learn
> and you would never grow.   —BEYONCÉ KNOWLES

THE PROMISE

The Ready State

The most valuable skill today is the ability to think and to manage attention. When you're in control of your attention, you are able to relax and apply the appropriate energy and focus to whatever it is that you are doing. It is then that you're in what we call the ready state.

The Ready State and You

What does *your* most focused and engaged state, your ready state, look and feel like? Let's start getting a better sense of it by identifying what it *isn't*.

WHAT DOES IT FEEL LIKE WHEN YOU ARE "OFF"?

Understanding what it feels like to be "off" can help you better identify when you're "on." While being "off" can be experienced in various ways, it has some consistent characteristics. "Off" may feel something like:

- *Anxious*
- *Stressed*
- *Failing*
- *Disappointed*
- *Nervous*
- *Overwhelmed*

Take two minutes, grab a blank sheet of paper, and make a list of all the things that you feel, experience, or sense when you are feeling "off."

WHAT DOES IT FEEL LIKE WHEN YOU ARE "ON"?

Feeling "on," or in what we call the ready state, is probably not as difficult to recognize, but it can certainly be harder to achieve. When you really feel as if things are clicking along, when life is moving in the right direction, when time is disappearing, when you're accomplishing your tasks, you're experiencing the **ready state**.

"On" may feel something like:

- *Empowered*
- *Independent*
- *Strong*
- *Focused*
- *Present*
- *Fearless*
- *Hopeful*

Take two minutes, flip over that same sheet of paper, and make a list of all the things that you feel, experience, or sense when you are "on," when you are in your ready state.

The ready state describes you at your best, for any situation.

A Ready State for Everything

The ready state doesn't have to be limited to your role as a student at school. In everything you do, you can do it best when you are focused, relaxed, and fully engaged, whether at your job, in sports, in friendships, or in life itself. Take a look at this list of ready states, and add any that are relevant to you.

READY STATES

Learning Ready	Relaxation Ready	Driving Ready
Homework Ready	Game Ready	Performance Ready
Service Ready	Vacation Ready	Finals Ready
School Ready	Job Ready	_____ Ready
Family Ready	Listening Ready	_____ Ready

Let's take a look at a few of these examples to show how the ready state applies to each.

What does it mean to be *learning ready*? The optimal state for learning is being focused on what is being taught (not distracted), relaxed, prepared with whatever materials you might need (not stressed), and engaged with the subject at hand so that you can synthesize, make connections, and apply your learning.

What does it mean to be *relaxation ready*? Optimal relaxation involves being focused on whatever leisure activity you have chosen (not distracted); relaxed physically, mentally, and emotionally (not stressed); and engaged with whatever activity you're involved with so that you can enjoy the benefits of downtime.

What does it mean to be *game ready*? Optimal gaming is being focused on the game at hand and your role in it (not distracted); relaxed and in peak performance, knowing that you are prepared (not stressed); and engaged fully with each moment so you can offer your best for yourself and/or your team.

What does it mean to be *homework ready*? Optimal studying means focusing on the work that has to be completed (not distracted); being relaxed, confident that you have the materials you need and the skills to complete the task (not stressed); and fully engaged to make the most effective and productive use of your study time.

Do you see the pattern? The ready state is one of focused, relaxed engagement, which enables you to bring your best to whatever it is that you are doing.

THE PRACTICE

Can You Get to a Ready State When Needed?

While everyone has experienced the feeling of being "on" at some point or other, GTD can offer the tools and behaviors needed to generate "on" as often as possible. If you are confident that you can always get back to a ready state, no matter what the circumstances, then you can enter into any and all situations without fear or worry, prepared to respond and make things happen.

Ready to Get Knocked *Out* of Ready?

Wouldn't it be great to always be in the ready state? The truth is that new challenges and complexities will appear constantly, and each one holds both opportunities for success and the danger of pitfalls.

If you play things incredibly safe, avoiding situations and opportunities that might make you uncomfortable or result in failure, whether activities, relationships, tryouts, or classes, you won't necessarily feel "on," but you might be able to avoid that feeling of "off," at least for a while.

Some young people go this route. They fully immerse themselves in the culture of distraction and do only the things they feel most comfortable doing. Some even numb themselves further with digital entertainment or even with drugs and alcohol. At first this withdrawn and numb state might be attractive. What could be easier than being left alone to play video games all day, eat junk food, and hang with friends? We all know deep down, though, that it wouldn't be truly fulfilling.

The truth is, no matter how much you intentionally avoid—or how much control you think you have right now in your life—challenges and pitfalls will undoubtedly force you to occasionally feel "off," become distracted, be overloaded, and feel overwhelmed.

Instead of helping you stay comfortable, we will instead encourage you to step out of comfortable, as often as possible. We urge you to fearlessly take risks, to engage with things that may stretch you or knock you out of your comfort zone, and force you "off."

If you have the skills and tools to always get back to "on," to return to your ready state, then you can confidently confront any situation with the knowledge that you can recover. You will always be ready—ready for whatever comes next. That's the principle of this book and the power of GTD: Take risks, get knocked off, and return to "on" with confidence.

Stuff

So far we've discussed connectivity, opportunities, and pitfalls and how these pitfalls can make you feel "off." We've described the optimal ready state and the two parts of the brain that play the most significant role in achieving that state, Myggy (the amygdala) and Cortland (the prefrontal cortex). We've explained that the key to maintaining the ready state is engaging both of these areas of the brain in partnership.

Why, then, can't you just *decide* to perfectly engage the different parts of your brain and feel ready all the time?

STUFF

Meet **stuff**.

Stuff is always coming. Stuff is not good or bad. Stuff just *is*. In learning to recognize stuff, you can learn to manage it well.

Stuff is anything that shows up in our world—physically, digitally, mentally, emotionally—that still requires some decision or action and has yet to be determined and isn't yet organized.

What Is All This Stuff?

Stuff takes many forms and can come from many different places. For example, it could take the form of a school assignment, dirty clothes on the floor, a tryout for a sport, an issue with your health, a broken skateboard, a conflict with a friend, a new club that is being offered at school, or a dreaded presentation you have to give. Stuff can be generated by outside sources or from within your own mind.

What types of stuff show up most often in *your* world? Where is it all coming from?

A Masterful Opponent

If stuff isn't dealt with effectively, it can very quickly make an impact on you—physically, mentally, emotionally, even spiritually.

 As your life gets more complex, the amount of stuff entering it increases and can be a source of constant distraction. It can keep you from feeling ready, force you to quickly lose focus and perspective, and knock you "off." If you aren't careful, stuff can run your life.

To more accurately define and understand "stuff," we can look back at a discovery from almost one hundred years ago, made by a woman named Bluma Zeigarnik. She discovered some interesting things about the brain and what she called **open loops**.

THE ZEIGARNIK EFFECT

Bluma Zeigarnik was a Russian psychologist in the early 1900s and one of the first Russian women to ever attend college. In 1927, she published some important research about the brain. Her work began one day while eating at a restaurant and watching the behavior of the servers.

She noticed that once diners finished their meal and paid their bill, it was quite difficult to get the attention of their server again. While most people might just assume that the servers were only interested in the remaining *paying* customers, Zeigarnik explored this further. What she discovered was that it wasn't just that the servers had stopped paying attention; once the customers paid their bill, the servers were much less likely to remember anything about their order. Although they could still easily recall the orders from the tables that were still being served, their brains had somehow "let go" of the completed orders.

She took this observation outside of the context of restaurants and did some additional investigating. What she discovered were some startling and important traits of the human brain. The **Zeigarnik Effect**, as it has come to be known today, states simply that the brain naturally remembers and holds on to anything that is interrupted or incomplete. These interruptions and incompletions are called open loops.

OPEN LOOP

The brain naturally seeks closure, or completion. Without it, part of the brain will hang on to the open loop until it is closed and there is completion. Nearly one hundred years later, this phenomenon is more relevant than ever.

This is easy enough to test for yourself. Have you ever had a thought that enters your consciousness more than once? Perhaps you've had it for several days, a week, or even a month or more. If you answered yes, you've experienced a good example of an open loop. For our purposes, an open loop is anything pulling at your attention that doesn't belong where it is, the way it is.

Are we related?

You do look familiar...

Stuff and Sleep

Let's look at a concrete example of the impact of open loops.

Have you ever had trouble falling asleep because you've had things on your mind? Those things that capture your attention are an open loop, a form of mental stuff.

Throughout any given day, stuff is continually coming at you. You have a lot of interactions, a lot to do, and a lot to keep track of. You get busy and preoccupied and may overlook certain tasks.

Let's say, for example, that you have a friend named Jasmine. Jasmine is absent from school because of sickness. You promise to share that day's math lesson. This is an example of an agreement between you and Jasmine, and because it is incomplete, it becomes an **open loop**.

As the day ends and your body is preparing to shut down and get some sleep, your brain also starts to rest and seek closure, and in doing so, it brings open loops back to your attention for resolution. You suddenly remember that you haven't honored the agreement you made with Jasmine, and sleep now became harder to achieve.

Remember, your amygdala does not have a sense of time. It wants resolution *now*. However, you obviously can't close all loops and finish everything while you lie in bed late at night. As a result, your brain nags you (and nags you, and nags you). Any agreements you've made or assignments that are coming due soon may come to your attention as you fall asleep.

Not only do the number of open loops tend to increase as you get older and things get more complex, but connectivity has *exponentially increased* the opportunity for them to show up. These open loops can, if not dealt with, build up and cause overload, which leads to stress and anxiety. Open loops, if not dealt with, can reappear at any time, which can cause distraction.

But what if you could learn to recognize stuff as soon as it enters your world and prevent it from ever becoming an open loop? What if you could learn to become familiar with the signals from your brain that identify those open loops, and in doing so quickly put them to rest?

GTD can help you learn to effectively deal with open loops and stuff *before* they begin to have a negative impact.

"Out of sight, out of mind" is not really out of mind, not at a deeper level.   —DAVID ALLEN

Control and Perspective

Achieving the ready state requires you to deal effectively with stuff—with open loops—and this is an ability that can be learned. To achieve the ready state, you need two things—appropriate *control* over and *perspective* on your stuff. The remainder of this book is dedicated to developing the skills and behaviors necessary to attain this control and perspective.

CONTROL

Control can mean a lot of different things.

In GTD, control does not refer to "control over." You don't have control over your own life or the life of anyone else, no matter how hard you try. Instead, we use "control" here to refer to stability, or "control within." This means that, given all of life's realities and your current circumstances and situations—all of life's stuff—you possess an element of control within it, called **operational control**.

Think of operational control as you do your role as the player of a video game. You don't have control over the gaming environment or what challenges come your way, as you're not the game designer. However, you *do* hold a controller in your hand, which allows you to decide what your character does within the environment. This is operational control.

What does operational control look like in everyday life? For example, while you don't control the amount of homework you are assigned, you *are* in control of how you engage with and handle it. You don't control whom the coach decides to play in the game, but you *are* in control of your own preparation, conditioning, and attitude. You don't control the parents you have, the financial situation you were born into, or your particular genetics, but you *do* have complete control of how you choose to engage with all those things.

GTD can help you optimize operational control over stuff. In doing so, you can learn to create the conditions for things to happen. You have the ability to create the conditions for effective homework practice, for your best tryout, for positive interactions with family, for responsibly managing your resources and finances.

Control can also help you create space in your mind so that you can think and imagine and clear space in your world so you can focus on the things that are most important to *you*.

PERSPECTIVE

Control is only the first part of the formula for achieving the ready state. You must also know *where* you are going and *why*. That's called perspective.

Perspective is the ability to look ahead, to see where you are going. Perspective is the vision, the "why" behind anything that you choose to do.

GTD can help you determine where you are and understand where your actions are leading you. It can help you decide what is important and what is not. It can help you dream big and create momentum toward those dreams.

Control + Perspective = Ready

If you have the tools and skills necessary to gain the appropriate control and perspective, you can always get back to the ready state—ready for now, ready for what comes next, and ready for whatever life presents. For a GTD'er, the cycle of moving between "on" and "off" states is natural and nonthreatening. This on/off dynamic is called the **surfboard effect**.

THE SURFBOARD EFFECT

Surfers are constantly looking for the next wave, which might hold the challenge they want or need. They thrive in this state of being on the edge of control and being out of control, where they can push the boundaries of their capabilities and creativity. It is in this state where time seems to disappear. They are in flow; they are in the moment.

When surfers enter the water, they mount their boards, their ankles strapped to a leash connecting them to the board. Waiting, they search the horizon for potential waves. Some are big; some are small. When the right one arrives, they paddle quickly, stand up on their board, and begin their ride, surfing on top of the chaotic water below. Sometimes they will continue on their ride until they reach a soft landing. Sometimes, as they push the boundaries of their creativity, they will wipe out. When they do, what piece of gear will help them get back on the board? The ankle leash.

ACHIEVE

MAINTAIN

REGAIN

Surfing is an especially good metaphor for GTD. When you have a lot of stuff coming at you, you can develop a system to surf above it all. GTD tethers you to a trusted system to help you navigate life, get back on your board, and catch another wave. Doing so enables you to harness the energy of whatever life throws at you, whether it ends smoothly or in a wipeout. Every time you begin surfing again, you get better with each run.

This describes the process of achieving control and perspective. The goal is not to be "on" all the time, always maintaining great control and perspective. Instead, you can enjoy "on" while it lasts and keep pushing yourself, knowing that stuff will occasionally knock you "off." When that happens, use the GTD tools and behaviors to get back to a ready state.

THE PRODUCTIVE HABIT

Let's preview the habits, tools, and skills that you will learn in this book that will enable you to achieve control and perspective.

Thinking Differently

You can train yourself with practice, like surfers, athletes, or musicians, to build good habits.

You can train yourself to be more proactive, responsive, and focused in managing the stuff that enters your life. You can learn to minimize the impact of open loops and get a lot more done with a lot less effort. To be more naturally productive, you need to develop productive habits. School and life will give you a wide variety of stuff for practice. Use it to your advantage.

Some of the GTD practices will seem unnatural at first. However, think back to the first time you tried riding a bike. At first, finding your balance was a clumsy process. After a bit of practice, it became more comfortable and eventually required little or no thought.

To gain control over stuff, you will learn how to (1) **capture** what has your attention; (2) **clarify** what each item means and what to do about it; (3) **organize** the results into categories; (4) **reflect** on and review what you have identified in each category, so you can (5) **engage** and do what needs to be done.

These are actual logical steps we all take any time we need to bring something under control.

They're simple enough in principle, but most people can greatly improve how they use them. The ability to gain control is only as good as the weakest link in this five-step chain. Let's take brief look at each of these Five Steps before digging more deeply into each one.

AN EMPTY HEAD: CAPTURE

One of the major shifts you'll make in your behavior in order to gain control will be learning to keep *nothing* in your head.

Trying to *mentally* keep track of all the stuff coming at you, at a historic time when the amount of information assaulting you is greater than any time in human history, is a recipe for disaster. Your brain was simply not designed to store hundreds of open loops. As a matter of fact, current research indicates that you can hold about four items in your working memory. Beyond that, the cognitive load begins to create drag and make you become less effective.

If you think about your day—classes, homework, activities, relationships, responsibilities, etc.—can you even estimate the number of things your mind might be trying to track? You *could* try to just remember it all, and you might actually be able to do so with relative success. But as complexity increases and eventually generates too much stuff, you'll likely experience some form of distraction and ultimately even overload.

The first step toward control is to offload all stuff—getting it out of working memory. Instead, you'll keep it all—whether physical, digital, or mental stuff—somewhere *other* than in your head. We call these locations—these simple storage spaces outside the mind—**buckets**.

This practice alone can be revolutionary. Once your brain experiences the relief of releasing all the stuff it has been trying to hold, it has the free space to attain a newfound

BEFORE   AFTER

control, with new levels of freedom and new opportunities for creativity. This first step is called **capture**.

DEALING WITH THE STUFF YOU GATHERED: CLARIFY

The second step involves a simple mental process for making decisions about all the stuff that you have gathered into buckets during step 1.

Making decisions is not a new or revolutionary concept. Making effective decisions, however, may require a few new skills, while making efficient and effective decisions with the least amount of effort is an art form. We call it the **fundamental thinking process**.

Carrying out this process results in the complete transformation of stuff into one of six distinct forms: **actions**, **projects**, **checklists**, **someday/maybe**, **reference**, and **trash**.

Effective and efficient decisions preserve valuable energy.

What if you could deal more effectively with your schoolwork and have more energy and space to pursue other passions? Learning to make smart decisions can achieve that. To successfully engage in this process, you will need to truly engage Cortland, the underutilized part of the brain. This step is called **clarify**.

PRESERVING DECISIONS: ORGANIZE

Have you ever lost something of value, an important assignment, password, or file that then required extra work from you to either find or re-create? We don't know of anyone who likes to do work they've already done all over again, as it's a waste of both time and energy.

Likewise, if you don't preserve the decisions you make, you'll eventually have to make them over again. To avoid that, the third step will show you how to set up simple lists, also called maps, to help keep a record of the work and decision-making that you will have done.

Step 3 is called **organize**.

MAP CHECKING: REFLECT

Once you have assigned things to their respective places and made some simple maps to preserve your decisions, the behavior that will keep you in control and help regain that control when you get knocked off-balance will involve slowing down for a few moments and doing simple map checks.

In navigational terms, maps keep you going in the right direction, reroute you if you run into trouble, and get you back on track if you get lost. In this step, you will learn about how to conduct daily and weekly reviews to keep you consistently heading in the right direction.

Step 4 is called **reflect**.

MAKE IT HAPPEN: ENGAGE

The final step toward gaining control is learning to effectively take action on what you have decided is important. There are some simple decision-making criteria that you can use to narrow your choices and make big gains. This is where you begin to see visible and physical progress. This is where you get to move and do.

Step 5 is called **engage**.

While the Five Steps might represent a shift in some habits and practice, you're likely doing them in some form already. Let's take a look at some simple examples of where these steps might occur naturally.

Everyday Examples

Take a simple example like the experience of trick-or-treating on Halloween. When kids head out to collect candy from neighbors, they begin by taking a bag or a pillowcase (bucket) with them to collect incoming candy (capture). Upon gathering the loot for the evening, they return home, dump out the bag, and count, identify, and sort the candy into buckets like good candy vs. bad candy, chocolate vs. fruity delight, etc. (clarify and organize).

On the more practical side, think about the process of doing laundry. People often set up a hamper or basket (bucket) in which to pitch their dirty clothes (capture). The dirty clothes are separated into whites, darks, and delicates (clarify), and they are sorted so they are ready to wash (organize). When it comes time to wash, they take a last quick look at the sorted piles (reflect) and then throw a load in the washing machine (engage).

Using these same Five Steps, you can find the appropriate control and focus no matter who you are, where you are, where you find yourself, or what you are facing.

I don't want other people to decide who I am.
I want to decide that for myself.   —EMMA WATSON

SUMMARY

We're facing more information and connectivity than ever before. While they offer amazing opportunities, the sheer number of inputs can lead to some pitfalls, which can result in feelings of stress, anxiety, and even depression. GTD is a new skill set to learn in order to thrive in this new age of connectivity.

The amygdala, the reactive part of the brain, and the prefrontal cortex, the analytical, decision-making part, are the two parts of the brain most relevant in this new age.

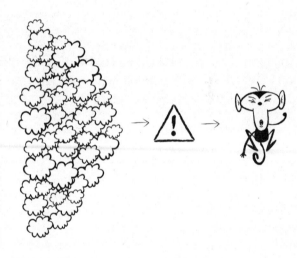

The **ready state** describes the optimal feeling of being "on" and requires both of these parts of the brain. This ready state involves finding the balance of **control** and focus. To achieve, maintain, or regain control and **perspective** involves learning to effectively deal with stuff. "Stuff" is the term used for everything that comes into your consciousness each day. If stuff isn't dealt with, it will remain in the form of **open loops**. Open loops can undermine control and perspective and can lead into the **pitfalls** of busyness, **distraction**, and **overload**.

Learning how to gain control and achieve freedom involves learning to effectively deal with stuff.

KEY TERMS

- Pitfall
- Overload
- Overwhelm
- Distraction
- Ready State
- Control
- Perspective
- Stuff
- Open Loop

QUESTIONS FOR THOUGHT OR DISCUSSION

- We all experience the pitfalls of overload and distraction at one time or another. Which of the pitfalls do you find yourself experiencing most often?
- What is the biggest source of distraction for you when your focus is needed?
- When you have a free moment, what do you tend to do? Where does your mind go?
- What gains do you experience when you are in the ready state? What do those close to you experience?
- What pains do you experience when you are not in the ready state? What do those close to you experience?
- What form of stuff most often shows up in your world? As of right now, how do you most often deal with it? How is that working for you?
- Do you ever have trouble falling asleep? If so, what keeps you awake at night?

Part 2
The Practice
of GTD

Don't find a fault; find a remedy.
Anybody can complain.   —HENRY FORD

GAINING CONTROL: THE FIVE STEPS

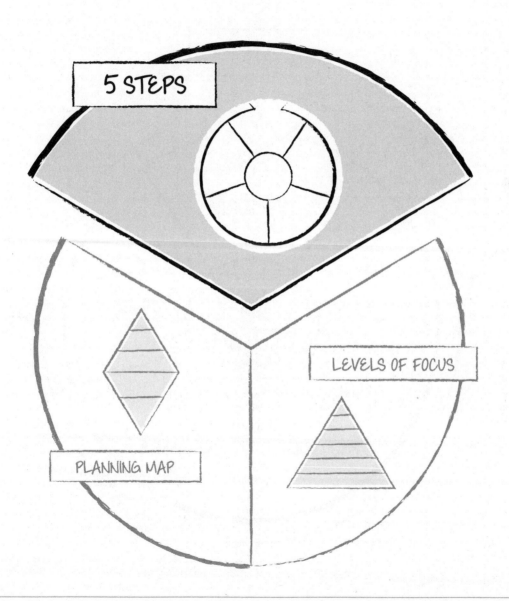

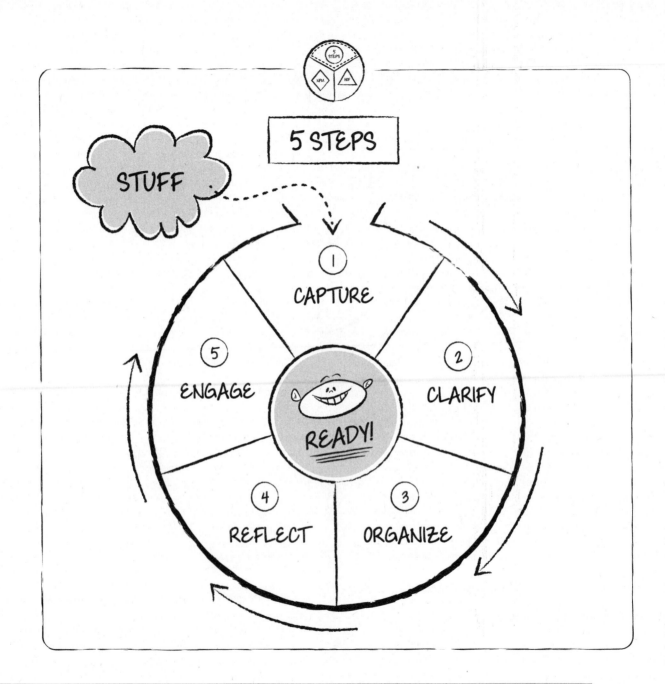

STEP 1: CAPTURE

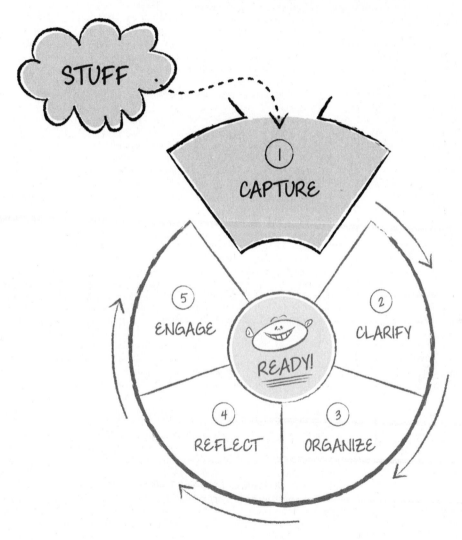

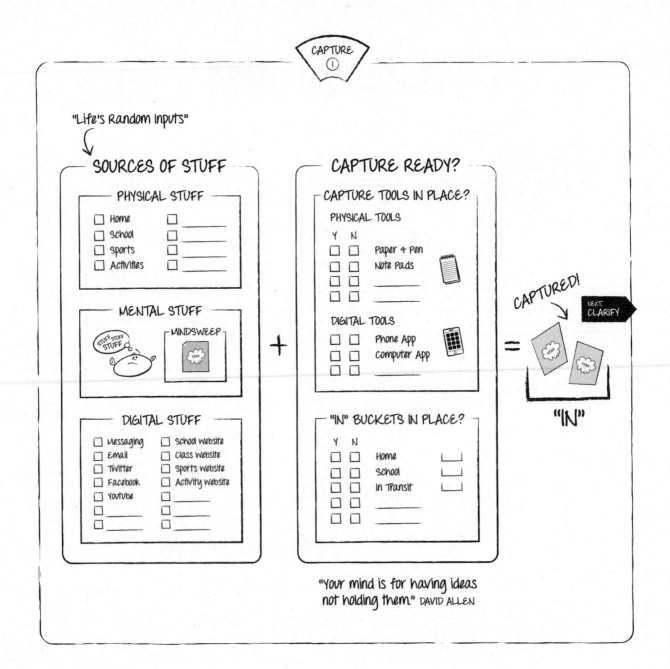

CAPTURE
①

"Life's Random Inputs"

SOURCES OF STUFF

PHYSICAL STUFF
- ☐ Home ☐ _____
- ☐ School ☐ _____
- ☐ Sports ☐ _____
- ☐ Activities ☐ _____

MENTAL STUFF
STUFF STUFF STUFF

MINDSWEEP

DIGITAL STUFF
- ☐ Messaging ☐ School Website
- ☐ Email ☐ Class Website
- ☐ Twitter ☐ Sports Website
- ☐ Facebook ☐ Activity Website
- ☐ Youtube ☐ _____
- ☐ _____ ☐ _____
- ☐ _____ ☐ _____

+

CAPTURE READY?

CAPTURE TOOLS IN PLACE?

PHYSICAL TOOLS

Y N
- ☐ ☐ Paper & Pen
- ☐ ☐ Note Pads
- ☐ ☐
- ☐ ☐

DIGITAL TOOLS
- ☐ ☐ Phone App
- ☐ ☐ Computer App
- ☐ ☐

"IN" BUCKETS IN PLACE?

Y N
- ☐ ☐ Home ☐
- ☐ ☐ School ☐
- ☐ ☐ In Transit ☐
- ☐ ☐ _____
- ☐ ☐ _____

"Your mind is for having ideas
not holding them." DAVID ALLEN

=

CAPTURED!

NEXT:
CLARIFY

"IN"

Oh Yeah . . . I Almost Forgot . . .

Have you ever been in a situation where you had to remember to bring something to school the next day? Perhaps an important assignment or a piece of sports equipment or a permission slip?

If so, what did you do with that item the night before to make sure that you didn't forget it?

You probably did something like putting it in your backpack or by the front door or next to your phone or keys—somewhere or next to something you were quite sure you *wouldn't* forget.

This is actually a brilliant strategy. Why? Because your brain is designed to notice patterns. You were alerted by your brain how important the item was, and then you figured that in the morning you'd likely be tired/hurried/distracted and feared you might forget it. You didn't trust your morning brain to remind you. By putting the item with something you knew you wouldn't forget, you used the prefrontal cortex of your brain to quiet your amygdala.

By doing so, you effectively let it go. You stopped worrying about it, which enabled you to move on and think about something else. You could sleep.

Get It Out!

Remember those pesky open loops that can wreak havoc on the brain? They appear because of all the incompletions or interruptions that enter your world each day, hour, minute, even second, all in the form of stuff. While your brain is an incredibly powerful tool, it simply wasn't designed to store stuff or open loops.

Your mind is for having ideas, not holding them.   —DAVID ALLEN

So, does that mean you have to close every open loop and immediately complete everything?

The answer is . . . *sort of.*

Your brain indeed desperately seeks closure, and in order to actually achieve that control in the face of an historic amount of stuff, you'll have to learn some new and different types of thinking to actually achieve that closure.

It is *not possible* to complete all the stuff that is continually coming your way. Some of the unhappiest people are those who spend all their time trying to stay on top of everything and finish it all. Making this attempt can result in a never-ending, unsatisfying grind. The truth is that as soon as you finish one assignment or chore or achieve a goal, another will appear. Waiting for the magical day of finally being "done" is fruitless. Control is ultimately impossible to achieve.

Some try to get *just enough* done so that they can make it to weekends or vacations or summer breaks. They do the least amount possible to keep their teachers or parents off their backs. This isn't control, either; it's escapism, and it, too, won't help you feel ready.

But what if you could feel calm and in control, even at the busiest time of the year? What if you could have a clear mind and no stress even though you still have a whole list of things you need to do?

What if teachers and parents were off your back, not because you were just getting by but because you have proven that you could manage it all on your own?

What would that feel like? How freeing might that be?

Intrigued? If so, we will introduce an alternative behavior to support the collecting and closing of loops.

This behavior is the first in a series of Five Steps, and it is called **capture**.

Capture can be described in two simple words: *GRAB IT.*

Biggest lie I tell myself: "I don't need to write that down.
I'll remember it."   —EVERYONE

Offloading

Capture: To gather, and at times generate, items and ideas identified as potentially meaningful, about which one has any attention or interest in possibly deciding or doing something

Your brain obsesses over open loops. It will see them, hear them, then file and hang on to them, and it will be ready to reintroduce them at the worst times.

You might suddenly remember you needed to bring something home from school right as you walk in the front door of the house.

You might remember that you needed to finish an assignment just as you walk into the classroom on the day it is due.

You might continually think about the need to get moving on drivers' ed classes but groan at the idea of starting that process.

You might panic about an important project you were supposed to have already started on right as you are trying to shut down for the day and fall asleep.

Unfortunately, **open loops** can haunt your brain, specifically the amygdala. Myggy has no mercy, no grace, no sense of context or time.

YOUR BRAIN WANTS CLOSURE.

So what can you do about this?

You can't shut stuff off.

You can't finish it all.

You can ignore it, but you know it will reappear, likely at a worse time.

The first step to better manage stuff is really quite easy: You can remove the burden of housing it in your brain. Instead, offload all those ideas, tasks, chores, projects, worries, errands, and dreams to somewhere outside your brain.

This can actually be as simple as it sounds. Is there a subject on your mind that your brain is constantly reintroducing? Did you have the same thought about it more than once today? This week? This month? If you answered "yes," this thought is a good example of stuff and a potential open loop you most likely need to close.

Recognize that signal from your brain for the gift that it is. If you ignore it, try to let it go, or mindfully calm yourself out of worrying about it, you may find short-term success and start thinking about something else. However, it won't go away, because the loop is still open, and you can count on your brain to bring it back to your attention.

Instead, deal with that stuff.

Grab it. Write it down, anywhere: On a Post-it. On a piece of paper. On a napkin. On your phone. On the wall. On the bathroom mirror. The point is to simply get it *out* of your head and *off* your mind by writing it down.

Next, put that piece of stuff, that open loop, in a trusted place, where it can be dealt with later.

This is not procrastination. This is intentionally using *another* part of the brain, a *different* part of the brain—specifically, the prefrontal cortex—to create a new behavior, a new habit. In capturing, you're setting yourself up to deal with stuff when *you* decide, rather than being at your amygdala's mercy.

While writing stuff down might seem like more work at first, this simple habit will, in the end, prove to be both the easiest and most effective way of actually dealing with stuff.

Think about it for a moment. All your stuff is currently being held *somewhere*.

What is your current system for remembering stuff and tracking open loops?

Do you keep it all in your head? Do you count on someone else, like your mom, to remind you of what you need to do and where you need to be? Do you sit back and hope it all just magically works out?

What would it feel like to have your mind *completely* free of stuff and yet be confident that the stuff will be managed successfully?

In order to capture all this stuff, we will introduce you to a few tools that will make up your **capture system**. These tools will help you be ready to capture any amount of stuff and at any time and in any location. We call this being **capture ready**.

The first new tool is called a **bucket**.

Bucket: A holding bin, either physical or digital, for incoming items still to be processed.

Buckets as Trusted Holders

Buckets come in many forms, shapes, sizes, and locations. They can be physical tools, such as a plastic tray, a box, or a designated spot on your desk. They can be digital ones, such as a to-do list on a computer or mobile device.

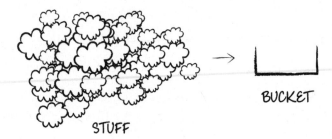

The form of the bucket, while an important decision, is not what's most important. Buckets that work for one person may not be effective for another. However, their function is exactly the same—keeping stuff out of your head. The process of figuring out what works best for you will be part of the fun.

Buckets are essentially just holding tanks. You want it to be easy to throw stuff into them for later, so place them in a location where capturing will be easy. A physical bucket should be able to hold different sizes of items—mail, registration forms, Post-its, books, etc. If your buckets aren't accessible and effective, your brain won't trust them and will continue to hang on to stuff, which defeats the entire purpose of this step.

How many buckets do you need? The overly simple answer is the least number that you can get away with to be able to successfully capture *everything*. It helps to think about the sources of your stuff. If you know where stuff is likely to come from, you can place a bucket there to catch it.

```
┌──────── PHYSICAL STUFF ────────┐
│  ☐ Home          ☐ _____    │
│  ☐ School        ☐ _____    │
│  ☐ Sports        ☐ _____    │
│  ☐ Activities    ☐ _____    │
└────────────────────────────────┘
```

Most will find that they need a minimum of three buckets: a designated bucket at home, a bucket at school/work, and a bucket to capture stuff while out and about and on the go.

At home, a bucket could just be a designated spot in your house where you can collect only incoming stuff to be dealt with later. Once you have it set up, let your family know about it. Tell them that if there is something that they want you to look at or that belongs to you, they should stick it in this bucket. You'll no longer have to search around the house for mail or papers or your phone. Everything that is yours that needs your attention should go in that one place. The more you use it, the more your brain will trust it and the freer your mind will be.

At school, you could try a folder in your backpack or a particular spot in your locker. Put everything in this bucket that comes at you throughout the day so that you can deal with it when you're ready.

The mind is not a vessel to be filled
but a fire to be kindled.   —PLUTARCH

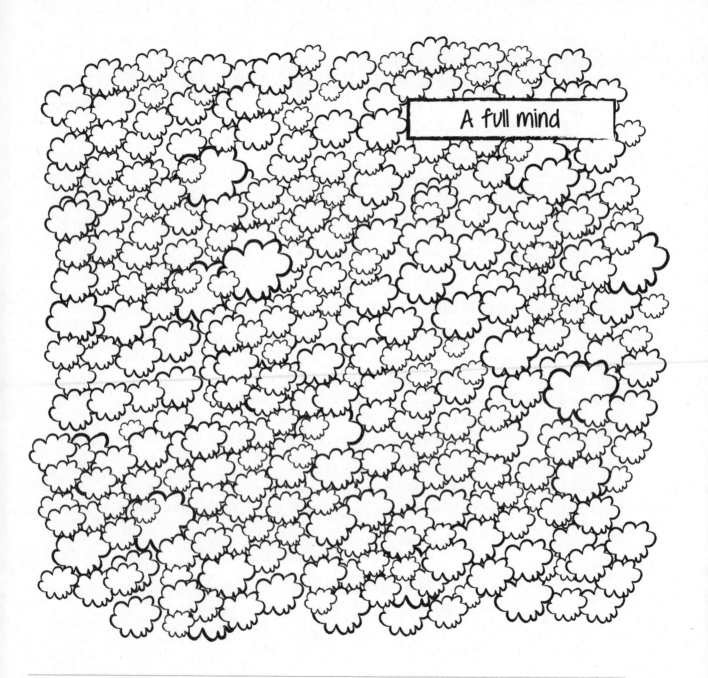

A full mind

A clear mind

CAPTURE TOOLS

Capture Tools

Sometimes stuff comes in physical form and can be placed right into a bucket—notes, mail, forms, bills, Post-its, etc. Many times, however, it comes in other forms, like a conversation, a direction from a teacher, a thought, an idea, or a task. This type of stuff exists only as thoughts in your brain. Give them physical form by writing them down with a **capture tool**, and then put them in a bucket for later.

Capture tools work best if they are readily available for use anywhere and at any time.

Hey Siri,
remind me...

Start deciding what sort of tool will work best for you by considering what you most often have with you. A purse with a notepad? A wallet with a small pen and paper? A phone with a list app? With a little bit of setup, you can turn any one of these items into an extremely effective capture tool.

If you invest a small amount of time setting up a few **buckets** and **capture tools**, and then use them to capture all the stuff that comes at you, your mind will learn to trust that all stuff will eventually be dealt with, and it can let go of the **open loops**.

In doing so, you become **capture ready**.

This is the first step toward **control**.

So, what do you need to do to become **capture ready**?

What tools do you already have?

What do you still need?

Test It Out!

To put this process to the test, try placing a capture tool in your bedroom. It could be as simple as a pad of paper and pencil next to your bed.

The next time you have trouble falling asleep, grab your capture tool and write down whatever's on your mind. You don't need to worry yet about *how* you write it down; write just enough so that when you look at it again, it is clear what it was that had your attention. Continue writing until you record it all. If something pops into your mind, write it down.

 Got a project coming up that needs your attention? Write it down. Worried about a test? Write it down. Have a conflict with a friend? Write it down. Did you have an opportunity to try something new? Write it down.

My bed is a magical place where I can suddenly remember everything I was supposed to do. —BILL MURRAY

Capture Ready Means Ready to Capture!

In order for the brain to learn to really let go and trust the capturing process, you'll have to get into the habit of capturing every open loop and piece of stuff that comes your way using

CAPTURE READY?

CAPTURE TOOLS IN PLACE?

PHYSICAL TOOLS

Y	N	
☐	☐	Paper & Pen
☐	☐	Note Pads
☐	☐	_____
☐	☐	_____

DIGITAL TOOLS

Y	N	
☐	☐	Phone App
☐	☐	Computer App
☐	☐	_____

"IN" BUCKETS IN PLACE?

Y	N		
☐	☐	Home	☐
☐	☐	School	☐
☐	☐	In Transit	☐
☐	☐	_____	
☐	☐	_____	

your capture tools and buckets. It's all or none in this process. If your brain doubts that you have captured it all, it will continue to be on heightened alert and actively scan for stuff.

The good news is that this practice is not as hard as it sounds. It takes some extra effort as you get started, but once you form the habit, you'll wonder why you ever tried to hold anything in your head at all. A clear mind feels so much better.

Let's get started on the actual capture process. The first step is to take account of all the stuff that has collected so far in your world. Depending upon how old you are and your habits up until this point, there could be quite a bit of older stuff. We call this **backlog**.

You likely will have physical stuff, digital stuff, and mental stuff to corral and capture. Let's start with your physical (analog) environment.

Head into your bedroom. Whether you have your own room or you share one, it's the place where you end your day, so set it up as your home base. Take a look around. Your room might be clean or messy, which is not important right now, as you can have a clean room with lots of stuff that needs your attention or a messy room with very little stuff that needs your attention.

You are going to engage in an activity called a **stuff hunt**, in which you'll search in these areas:

1. Physical space
2. Digital space
3. Mental space

Stuff hunt: An activity that involves intentionally scanning your physical, digital, or mental environment for anything that isn't reference, equipment, decorations, or supplies and might need your attention.

STUFF HUNT

STUFF HUNT—PHYSICAL SPACE

Your only job on a stuff hunt is to gather into your bucket anything that fits the definition of "stuff." You are searching for anything that might need your attention because it might require action, because it isn't where it should be, or because it's just trash. You're not going to actually *do* anything with whatever you find. For now, just collect it all in your bucket.

WARNING! BEWARE! The pitfall of distraction is likely to appear all throughout this activity! Stay focused. Put stuff in the bucket. That's your job.

As you scan your room, there are five types of items to notice. To help remember them, use the acronym REDS:

PITFALL

1. **Reference:** Information or materials you don't need right now but may need later. Reference items include things like books, magazines, your driver's license, etc.
2. **Equipment:** Tools/items that you regularly use or that serve a function. Equipment includes things like a clock, phone, computer, furniture, chargers, etc.
3. **Decoration:** Decoration doesn't serve a functional purpose but reflects your unique personality. Decoration includes items like photos, artwork, mementos, a bulletin board, etc.
4. **Supplies:** Practical things you use and can get used up. Supplies include things like paper, pencils, Post-its, highlighters, etc.
5. **Stuff:** Anything that is not REDS is stuff. It needs to go into your bucket.

STUFF SCAN

Scan the room for anything that isn't REDS and is therefore stuff. Stuff could include everything from incomplete homework assignments to permission slips to dirty clothes. If you can't put the physical piece of stuff in your bucket because of its size or location, write a word or words to represent the item on a piece of paper, and put that paper in a bucket (for example, "dead mouse in closet," "broken chair," "Mom's birthday"). When you look at that paper later, you will want to have written just enough to know what and where the relevant stuff is. If you are representing a piece of stuff by writing it down, use one piece of paper for each item. (This will be helpful in step 2.)

Take your time on the stuff hunt. Start with a quick scan of the room and capture the obvious items; then delve deeper into less visible places like drawers, closets, countertops, floors, shelves, backpacks, or anywhere that may contain stuff—especially if this is your first attempt at a scan.

Once you've placed it all in a bucket, the journey toward control has officially begun.

How do you feel as you're doing this? Don't worry yet if your feelings are positive or negative, as both of these are quite natural at this point in the process. Just pay attention to what you're feeling so that as you continue putting these tools and activities to the test you can notice shifts, changes, and ideally some wild improvements.

If, following a stuff hunt, everything in the room is now REDS and all the stuff that needs attention has been placed in a bucket, then for your brain, this is as organized as a room can possibly get. The space may not be neat and tidy, but it is truly *organized*, because everything is in the *exact place* that matches its *meaning*. You truly "cleaned" the room, and yet you haven't done anything except capture a bunch of stuff into a bucket.

If you look now at your space, it's what we call clear, because nothing else requires your attention and you have put everything you do need to deal with in a bucket that will be handled in step 2. For now, it is organized appropriately.

Now, before we get too excited and start giving one another pats on the back, you might actually have a bucket that is shockingly overflowing. That's completely okay, because we are just getting started. During the first time through, you have the potential for capturing a lot of stuff. As you get in the habit of doing a capture on a regular basis, the amount of stuff becomes less.

After you've completed a stuff hunt of your bedroom, think about any other places in your physical world that could benefit from the process. A kitchen counter? Your backpack?

Your locker or sports bag? A closet? A car?

STUFF HUNT—DIGITAL SPACE

Next, let's shift into your digital world, where we will conduct another stuff hunt. For some of us, the digital world may involve a brief scan, while for others, it will be a much more complicated and involved process than the one we did in physical space. It can be challenging to corral and capture digital stuff, because it can so easily hide within folders, within apps, or in the cloud. However, invisible stuff is *still* stuff, and your brain handles it in the same way.

Here is a recommended method of attacking this world:

Start by identifying the places where your digital stuff is currently generating and gathering. Some examples could be messaging accounts, school websites, a camera roll, or social media feeds.

Once you know *where* to conduct the digital stuff hunt, the next step is to decide *how* to capture the stuff from your digital world. You could use the same physical bucket and capture tool you used for your room. If that's the case, have your capture tool by your computer or phone and sit near your bucket. As you come across stuff that needs your attention, jot a note on a piece of paper describing the stuff and then drop it in your bucket. Items might include things like messages that need a response, files that need organizing, items to purchase, etc.

You could also decide to make a list or create a folder on your digital device as a form of a digital bucket and capture tool. If you choose to go this route, find a good program or app to do so. There are many list-managing apps available for download, or one may have already come preinstalled on your mobile device (Reminders, Notes, Tasks, etc.).

Don't overthink your choices of buckets and capture tools right now. The decisions you make don't have to be permanent ones. After you go through this process for the first time, you will likely figure out some things that are working well and some that aren't, and then you can adjust accordingly. Another one of the great things about GTD is that you change and interchange tools at any time. Your buckets and capture tools may change *forms*, but they *function* the same.

Go through each of your digital inboxes, your desktop, and any old files and folders, and search for any stuff that may hold meaning or need some attention or action. Look through your hard drive, your camera roll, your messages, your files on Google Drive, your social media feeds, class websites, calendars, etc.

You can then drag, drop, or capture each of those items into the predetermined digital bucket, or use your capture tool to jot them down and *then* put them into your bucket.

How is capturing in the digital world similar to or different from how you felt doing a stuff hunt in your room?

STUFF HUNT—MENTAL SPACE

Gathering up all your physical and digital stuff is a great start toward gaining control. There is, however, one location we have not yet deeply scanned for stuff, a place notorious for storing and even generating tons of open loops: your own brain.

Your brain can be the trickiest area to scan because it is the hardest to physically see, but it is also the most convenient to scan because it is the most accessible. Your brain is always with you, always scanning your world for potentially meaningful and relevant information, always hyperaware of incoming stuff, perhaps even generating its own stuff. Some of these items might represent open loops.

For example, let's say you just saw a notification for a drivers' ed registration deadline, and that reminds you that you have to talk to your parents about signing up for it. You have two choices regarding this new loop: 1) You *could* write it down in hopes of giving yourself the best opportunity to successfully manage it; or 2) Alternatively, you *could* just assume you'll remember it later. While you might save five seconds by not capturing this thought, it's important to realize that you also run the risk of both forgetting it and having Myggy remind you at the wrong time, perhaps as you are trying to study, or at three in the morning when you are trying to sleep, or perhaps the day after the deadline. In the end, the path of least resistance will be capturing.

If you want to unearth the stuff that your mind is holding on to so that you can deal with it on your terms, when *you* want to, try slowing down, put away your phone for a few moments, and let your mind just wander . . . and think. In those quiet moments, where does you mind go?

Wherever it lands, it will likely stumble onto an open loop, a piece of stuff. There is an activity that can help foster this mining process for open loops. It's like a stuff hunt for the brain and is called a **mind sweep**.

Mind sweep: An activity that involves capturing anything and everything that is on your mind or has your attention.

You can fool everyone else,
but you can't fool your own mind.

—DAVID ALLEN

Conducting a Mind Sweep

A mind sweep can act like a laxative for a backed-up brain.

To reveal the stuff that has collected in your brain using a mind sweep, grab some paper to serve as a capture tool. We recommend trying this on paper instead of on a device for at least the first couple of times to reduce the potential distractions from apps, alerts, and notifications. It can also be helpful to find a space where you know you can have a few minutes without being interrupted.

Start by just paying attention to what has your attention. What is on your mind? What is your brain bringing to your attention? What are you thinking about?

Whatever it is that you discover is on your mind, write it down on the piece of paper. You're removing the burden of tracking it from your brain by doing this. Don't worry yet about how you write it or what it is you have to do; just get it out by recording in some way, shape, or form.

At this point in the process, you are not trying to decide where or how to *focus* your attention; you are just determining what *has* your attention. If it is on your mind, it probably requires at least *some* additional thinking.

Your list might resemble something like this:

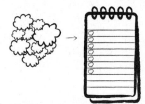

- Finals
- Prom
- Mom
- Retreat
- Gas money
- Driver's license
- Summer job
- Closet
- Volleyball
- New clothes

Paper is to write things down that we need to remember.
Our brains are used to think.
                                                    —ALBERT EINSTEIN

Trigger List

The first few minutes of a mind sweep will help you capture your active thoughts. But your brain also holds onto things at a deeper level, loops that aren't *actively* on your mind. Myggy might be ready to reintroduce these at the worst possible times.

To help dig deeper into your mind and search for more stuff, there's a companion tool for the mind sweep called a **trigger list**. A **trigger** is anything that serves as a reminder. Triggers can come in the form of an alarm on your phone, a Post-it note on your door, a message sent to yourself, etc. Triggers are meant to get you thinking about the right thing at the right time. A trigger list is a collection of triggers meant to stimulate your thinking at the right time. In a mind sweep, a trigger list is meant to help encourage thinking about stuff that maybe isn't quite as obvious. For the purpose of helping you with this initial deeper mind sweep, here is a sample trigger list developed by a teenager.

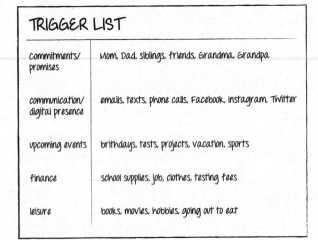

TRIGGER LIST	
commitments/ promises	Mom, Dad, siblings, friends, Grandma, Grandpa
communication/ digital presence	emails, texts, phone calls, Facebook, Instagram, Twitter
upcoming events	birthdays, tests, projects, vacation, sports
finance	school supplies, job, clothes, testing fees
leisure	books, movies, hobbies, going out to eat

To use the trigger list, spend about five minutes reading and thinking through each of the items, called triggers, on the list. If a trigger causes your mind to go to an open loop or it leads your thinking to other stuff, write it down. Capture any extra loops that present themselves on your same mind sweep list, and then put the list into your bucket.

Achieving Your First Inventory

The first time you go through the capture process is the most dynamic. If you think about it, you are attempting to achieve a complete initial inventory of *all* the stuff that has gathered in your entire life up until this very moment. That's a big backlog.

Thankfully, after you've finished this initial complete capture, all of your backlog will be in buckets and things will get easier. The goal from here on will be to continually capture the stuff that enters your world *as it arrives* and place it in your buckets.

Remember the surfboard effect? This is that first part—*achieving* control—working to get on top of that chaotic wave.

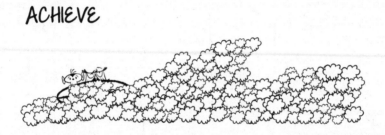

Achieving a complete inventory will take some time and patience. *Maintaining* and *regaining* control over stuff isn't nearly as involved, and once you've established the habit of being capture ready, this step gets way easier and becomes much more natural.

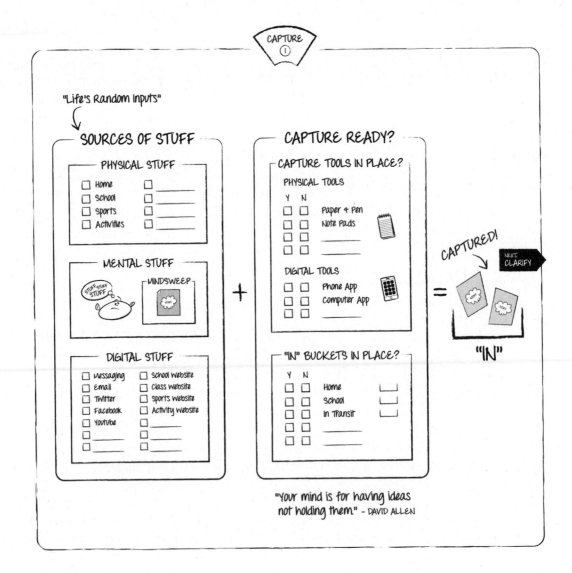

Stress or Relief?

If you've captured a complete inventory of stuff in your physical, digital, and mental worlds, you're likely to be experiencing some sort of reaction or emotional response to seeing it all in one place. Some people feel increased levels of *stress* and overwhelm at realizing how much needs their attention, and they feel tension, overload, and stress. If you have this reaction, remember that nothing you've captured in this process is *new*: It has remained there since it first became part of your world. This process simply helps you see it. Going through the next few steps will enable you to *transform* all this stuff, and you'll find a newfound control on the other side.

Other people feel an increased level of *relief*. Now that they see the full picture—a complete inventory backlog containing all the stuff they have to deal with—they realize that in reality their stuff isn't nearly as overwhelming as they feared it might be. Control is now within sight and attainable, and this creates an empowering sense of confidence. In fact, most people who take part in the process experience some mixture of both stress *and* relief.

The next step in the process is **clarify**, the secret sauce that can put you in the driver's seat. It will generate the operational control we have been describing, and it is the key to generating the ready state. It's time to truly get your prefrontal cortex *fully* involved, in perhaps brand-new ways.

SUMMARY

The first step toward getting stuff off your mind is to capture it. Capturing involves grabbing physical, digital, or mental items and externalizing them using **capture tools**. Placing captured stuff in trusted **buckets** will ensure that your mind trusts you will look at and deal with it at a later time. Capturing can close **open loops** even if action has yet to be taken or completion has yet to be achieved.

KEY TERMS

- Capture
- Bucket
- Stuff Hunt
- REDS
- Mind Sweep
- Trigger List
- Backlog

QUESTIONS FOR THOUGHT OR DISCUSSION

- Do you ever have trouble falling asleep? If so, what keeps you awake at night?
- What **capture tools** already exist in your world? Mailboxes? Inboxes?
- Have you ever made a to-do list? If so, what was your experience with it? What was helpful? What didn't work?
- Where do you think you need to set up **buckets** in your world to capture stuff? What is the least number you think you can get away with and still **capture** everything?
- Are you **capture ready**? Do you have tools (e.g., notepad, phone capture app) in place that will allow you to capture at any time? What other tools might you need or want?
- What form of stuff most often shows up in your world? As of right now, how do you most often deal with it? How is that working for you?

STEP 2: CLARIFY

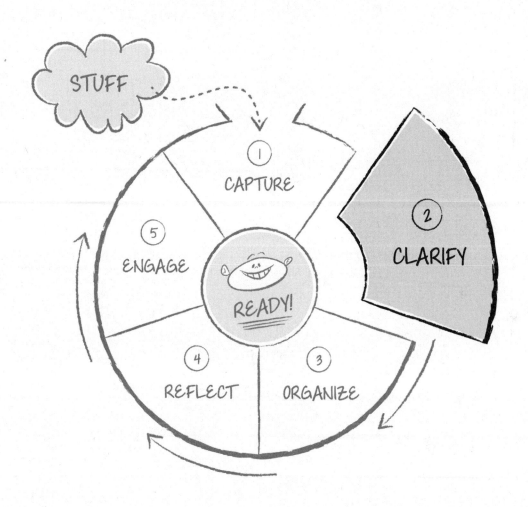

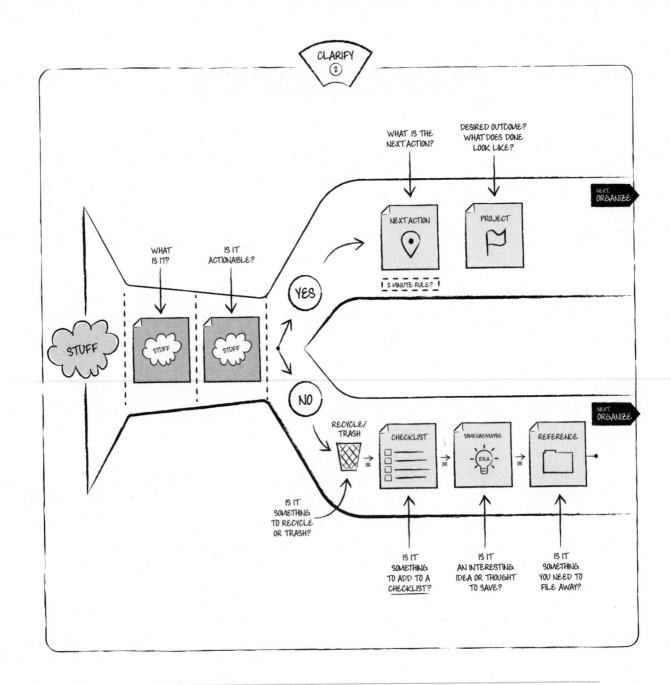

CLARIFY
②

WHAT IS THE
NEXT ACTION?

DESIRED OUTCOME?
WHAT DOES DONE
LOOK LIKE?

NEXT
ORGANIZE

NEXT ACTION

PROJECT

2 MINUTE RULE?

WHAT
IS IT?

IS IT
ACTIONABLE?

YES

STUFF

STUFF

STUFF

NO

NEXT
ORGANIZE

RECYCLE/
TRASH

OR

CHECKLIST

OR

SOMEDAY/MAYBE

IDEA

OR

REFERENCE

IS IT
SOMETHING
TO RECYCLE
OR TRASH?

IS IT
SOMETHING
TO ADD TO A
CHECKLIST?

IS IT
AN INTERESTING
IDEA OR THOUGHT
TO SAVE?

IS IT
SOMETHING
YOU NEED TO
FILE AWAY?

MAKE A DECISION

Clarify: To determine the exact meaning of something that emerged from the capture phase.

Clarify is not a visible step like capture. When you are capturing, there are mainly observable and tangible things you find or recognize as stuff, and you can see the results of your capturing in a bucket.

The clarify step, in contrast, is 100 percent mental. It involves decision-making and careful thinking. Clarify, however, is actually the most important and empowering of all Five Steps. It has consistently proven to be the most challenging for people, yet it is also the most profound. Once you have mastered this process, it never changes. If you really want to be ready, to gain control, to create some space in life for what you love, to find freedom, to change the world, to become invincible, to fly to the moon, to develop superpowers, start by learning how to practice and use this simple decision-making step.

THIS IS MY BIG OPPORTUNITY!

Think Once

So far you've taken step 1 and have done an initial corralling of all your stuff. Step 2 *deals* with all those items that have been captured. You will now learn how to deal with each of them, one at a time, one decision at a time.

OH NO... THIS LOOKS HARD... I BETTER GO FIND SOME DISTRACTION...

The clarify process will transform everything in your buckets from blobs of stuff into actionable, usable, or manageable forms. This is an absolute game changer and requires more focused attention than any other step. While a mind sweep is relatively fast and easy, clarify is slow and methodical. It is very much a mechanical process, and once you practice it for a while, it will become as automatic as brushing your teeth.

Pitfalls will continually attempt to wreak havoc during this step. Many people will actually *choose* to engage with sources of distraction instead of engaging with the step of clarify.

Why would anyone choose a **pitfall**? Because checking texts or playing video games spares you from having to do deep thinking and can provide a temporary sense of escape and relief. Thinking requires attention, space, and some effort, but the ultimate goal here is to think both effectively *and* efficiently. This means that you won't have to think more than you need to, because you won't end up having to think over and over later about something you procrastinated about today.

In other words, thinking *at the right time* prevents *wasted* time, *wasted* energy, and *wasted* attention, and it will create the conditions for clarity, momentum, freedom, clear space, and more energy for the things *you* want to do. It is the key to control. Clarify is the ultimate twenty-first-century skill.

Thinking is the hardest work there is, which is probably the reason why so few engage in it.　　—HENRY FORD

The Transformer Tool

Clarify involves taking a single piece of stuff that has entered your world and putting it through a thinking process. To help visualize and simplify this concept, we've created a tool known as the **transforming tool**.

The transforming tool isn't an actual physical tool. Its working component is called the *fundamental thinking process*. The image of the transformer tool included here is simply a model to help train your brain in this process.

When picturing how the transforming tool works, imagine that stuff enters the process from the left. It is assessed by asking a few questions, then sorted into one of two paths. As it continues along these paths, it is transformed into something new, something easier, and something more usable. This tool can work to transform anything that enters your life, and we mean *anything*.

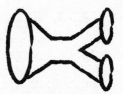

TRANSFORMER
TOOL

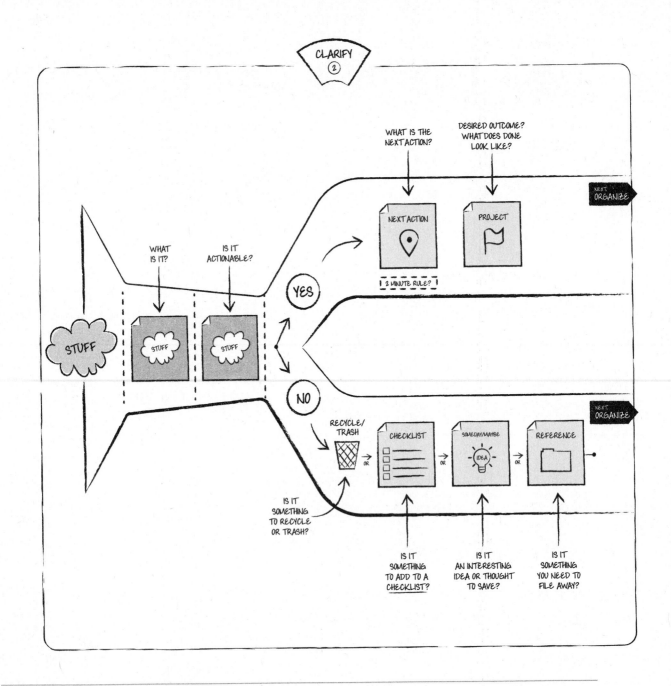

CLARIFY
2

WHAT IS THE
NEXT ACTION?

DESIRED OUTCOME?
WHAT DOES DONE
LOOK LIKE?

NEXT
ORGANIZE

NEXT ACTION

PROJECT

WHAT
IS IT?

IS IT
ACTIONABLE?

YES

2 MINUTE RULE?

STUFF

STUFF

STUFF

NO

NEXT
ORGANIZE

RECYCLE/
TRASH

CHECKLIST

SOMEDAY/MAYBE

IDEA

REFERENCE

OR

OR

OR

IS IT
SOMETHING
TO RECYCLE
OR TRASH?

IS IT
SOMETHING
TO ADD TO A
CHECKLIST?

IS IT
AN INTERESTING
IDEA OR THOUGHT
TO SAVE?

IS IT
SOMETHING
YOU NEED TO
FILE AWAY?

One Thing at a Time: What Is It?

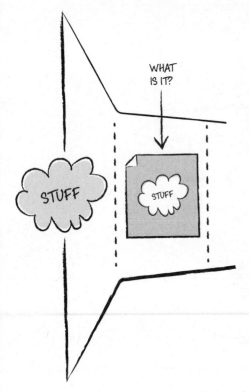

WHAT IS IT?

STUFF

STUFF

The way this decision-making process, and the transforming tool model itself, works is by taking one item of stuff at a time out of your bucket and asking the question "What is it?"

Begin by just answering that simple question. Don't overthink it—you're just allowing the item to trigger your memory and recall the nature of this piece of stuff and why it was captured.

Your answers might be something like these:

"This is my math homework."

"This is an invitation to a party."

"This is the receipt for my prom dress."

"This is an idea for how to cure cancer."

Once the stuff has been identified, it's time to engage in a higher-level thinking process about it. What follows are some sub-questions that will help make this as easy as possible.

IS IT ACTIONABLE?

Asking the question "Is it actionable?" will help you determine if the piece of stuff requires any action on your part and will sort every piece of stuff into one of two categories. "Is it actionable?" determines whether there is something you actually need to *do* with the stuff in question. This could mean acting on it right away or doing something with it on a later specific day or at a specific time.

The good news is that there are only two answers to this question.

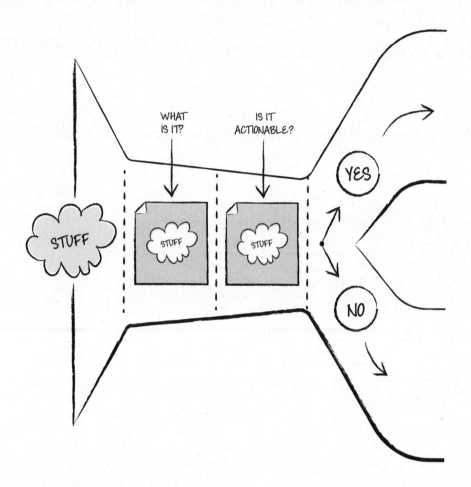

YES—This is something I will need to do, tend to, attend, turn in, complete, think about, research, look up, play with, talk to, message with, etc.

or

NO—This is something that I don't need, or I need/want to keep it, but it still doesn't require me to take any action on it at this time.

NONACTIONABLE ITEMS

Let's start with items for which the answer to the "Is it actionable?" question is no.

If an item is *not* actionable, meaning there is nothing you need to currently do with it, then it will take one of four forms: trash, checklist, someday/maybe, or reference.

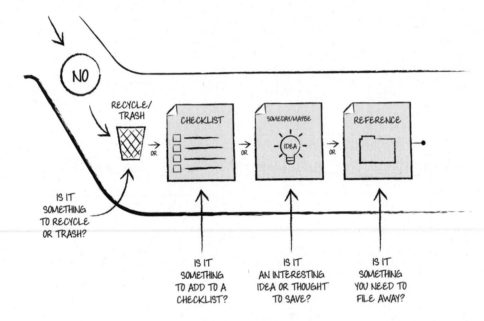

To decide which of these is the right choice, all that is needed is a clear understanding of exactly what each of these terms means. We specify *clear* and *exactly* here, because if you only have a vague sense of what these words actually mean, deciding which category each nonactionable item falls into can result in a slower and more difficult process. Let's carefully define each of these categories to make this process as easy as possible.

Nonactionable Category #1—Trash

Trash: Any nonactionable item that is unneeded and unwanted.

"Trash" doesn't necessarily mean "garbage." An old candy wrapper is garbage, which is a simple concept for your brain to grasp. When using our new definition of "unneeded" or "unwanted," however, some forms of trash can be a bit trickier to recognize.

Here are some questions to help determine if an item is trash:

- Will I truly use it or need it again?
- Do I have multiples of the item?
- Could I access this item online if I needed it?
- Are there any consequences if I don't have it in the future?
- Does the item hold any emotional or sentimental value?

If there is no solid argument as to why you would need something later, it is likely trash.

Hit the delete key, or place it in the garbage can or recycling bin or organics bin or wherever would be the best place to deposit that item, but acknowledge that it is genuinely trash, so that your mind can comfortably let it go.

An old assignment? Trash. A magazine you have already read? Trash. Junk emails? Trash.

By deleting these from your world, you remove them from your mind.

Nonactionable Category #2—Checklist

Checklist: A personalized list, developed over time, to assist with a specific activity.

Another type of nonactionable item that could result from the think- **CHECKLIST** ing process is a checklist.

A checklist is another form of a trigger list. Checklists contain triggers for specific situations or describe a collection of steps necessary for success. Checklists can serve you in many situations, such as knowing items to pack, things to do before you go somewhere, or the steps you need to take to be ready for a test.

Checklists can be made for a routine or procedure that happens repeatedly. They don't *require* any action, though they often contain a list of previous decisions and actions that have proven to result in success but haven't yet become habit. In creating a checklist, you have an opportunity to save time and make life easier for yourself down the road. This process saves you the *energy* of having to make the same decisions later and saves loads of future *time* on carrying them out.

The military uses checklists for tactical maneuvers. The police department uses checklists for protocols and procedures. Surgeons use checklists to prepare for surgery.

Where might *you* benefit from the power of a checklist? Say you have to pack for a three-night trip for school. You have to make a lot of little decisions before you go and remember a bunch of things to pack in order to make the trip go smoothly, from sleeping clothes to toothbrushes to phone chargers. The first time you go through this process of packing, you might need to spend quite a bit of time thinking through all these decisions. Or perhaps you don't spend enough time doing so, and you get to your destination and you realize you're missing some key items. There could be *huge* benefits on your *next* trip if you save a list of the things you packed on the earlier one, adding to it the things you forgot. Doing this turns your thinking into a checklist. A packing checklist will enable you to pack that much faster and more effectively in the future.

Checklists can support a wide variety of activities, but all offer the advantages of "pre"-thinking and save time and energy on "re"-thinking. Some sample checklists that might be generated in the clarify step are:

- Before Leaving for School checklist
- Lacrosse Equipment checklist
- Christmas Gift checklist
- Returning to School after Summer Vacation checklist
- Studying for Test checklist

There are a number of checklists that you can test out in Part 3 of this book if you are looking for more opportunities.

Nonactionable Category #3—Someday/Maybe Lists

Someday/Maybe: Anything that you may want to take action on later but doesn't require any action now.

SOMEDAY/MAYBE

Are there things that you would like to do at some point, but you don't ever really *have* to do them? These items likely fit into a category called someday/maybe.

Someday/maybe items don't *require* any action but are things you may indeed want to take on someday, if the conditions are right. In recognizing and keeping someday/maybe items, you can create potential opportunities for payoff later.

Someday/maybe items range from things like movies to see, books to read, trips to take, or wish lists to create to bucket list items like skydiving, climbing Mount Everest, going to Rome, playing in the NBA, or going to college. For example, when summer vacation begins, wouldn't it be fun to look at a collection of movies you decided you'd like to watch with friends or scan a list of books you collected and might like to take with you to the beach?

Identifying items as someday/maybe is a huge relief for the brain. You aren't deciding to *never* take action on these things, but instead you are cognitively placing them in a category that just says "not now." This allows these ideas to percolate and grow and develop and also relieves the pressure and guilt that can come with procrastination.

Later, when you have some extra time, control, and clear space through the Five Steps, you may find that you can move on these things creatively in a way that you couldn't before.

But while procrastination is a vice for productivity,
I've learned—against my natural inclinations—
that it's a virtue for creativity.   —ADAM GRANT

Nonactionable Category #4—Reference

Reference: Anything nonactionable that may be needed at a later time.

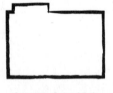

REFERENCE

Reference describes items that are nonactionable but *could* be needed later.

Reference materials can include things like directions, receipts, warranties, a class syllabus, a driver's license, passwords for websites, etc. These might be useful at some point, and not having the item might require some time and energy later if you need to find it.

Once you recognize stuff as reference and know you will need to keep it, the natural question that follows is "Where do I put it?" Hang on to that question. In step 3, Organize, we will set up some tools to help you store reference materials easily and effectively. For now, our focus is on helping your brain decide what category each item of stuff falls into.

Nonactionable Item Map

To review the process so far, take a look back at the **transforming tool**. Each piece of stuff goes through the *fundamental thinking process*, and the nonactionable items come out as **trash**, **checklist**, **someday/maybe**, or **reference** items.

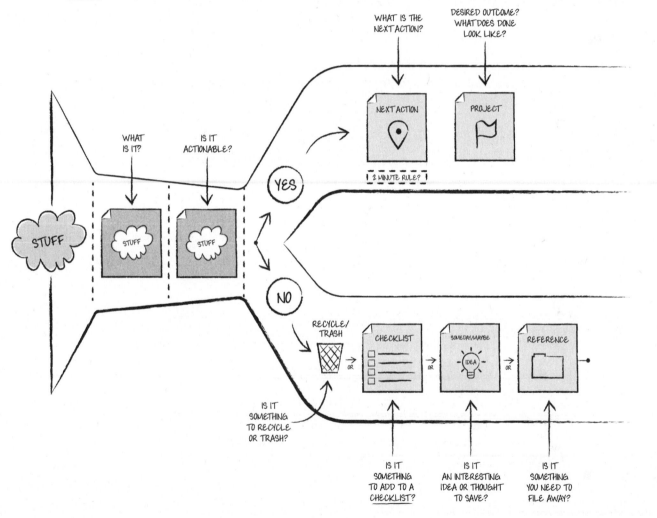

ACTIONABLE

You've seen that there are only four forms stuff can take if it is nonactionable. Now, let's take a look at what happens if the answer to the question "Is it actionable?" is yes. If there is something to *do* with the item, then there are two relevant categories: **next actions** and **projects**.

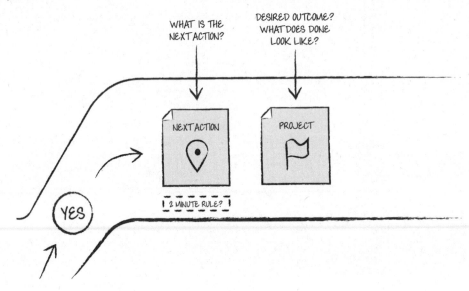

Actionable Category #1: The Next Action

Next Action: The next physical, visible activity that progresses something toward completion. This is what "doing" looks like.

The **next action** describes the single next physical, visible step in making progress on anything. "Physical" meaning that you have to take a specific action, involving actual movement. "Visible" means that you could be seen doing it if someone was watching you.

Some examples of next actions:

- Answer the review questions on page 12.
- Call Norah and ask about prom.
- Text Tyrell the directions to the tournament.
- Read chapter 4.

Sometimes the next action to take is obvious. When this is the case, you might end up taking a number of action steps without needing to do much clarifying. For example, the next actions to complete a homework assignment may be quite obvious to you because you have completed so many assignments before.

However, when a **next action** is *not* obvious, it can result in stress or procrastination. Have you ever felt stuck on something? Have you ever put something off because it seemed overwhelming or confusing? This is where the power of the next action can make all the difference in the world.

> Things rarely get stuck because of lack of time. They get stuck because the doing of them has not been defined. —DAVID ALLEN

The Power of the Next

There is nothing that people have ever done or have ever created that didn't begin with a single action. For an idea to become a movement, for inspiration to become a song, for a vision to become a painting, for a wonderful story to become a movie, for a three-point shot to go through the hoop, someone made a decision on what achieving the desired outcome would look like and then took the next action toward realizing it.

So many wonderful ideas end up dying a slow death because a single next action is never identified. Likewise, many ideas that at first seem crazy and impossible actually come to life when carried out with enough next actions.

Do you have things in your life that you wish were true but aren't? Do you have things you'd like to achieve but haven't? Do you have passions you'd like to pursue but aren't? Do you have a crazy idea that you'd like to attempt but haven't?

The ability to make things happen begins with identifying and moving on a single next action. Let's take a look at how to make these powerful next action decisions.

Procrastination

Have you ever found yourself putting something off over and over again or grumbling at the idea of getting started on something? Have you ever thought about *why* you might be feeling that way?

While it's true that there are sometimes unpleasant tasks that require some grit and effort, one of the most common reasons for procrastination is that the appropriate next action has yet to be determined. Sometimes we *think* we know what we need to do, but we continue to procrastinate.

If you find yourself in this situation, one thing to consider is whether you've actually identified the next action. More often than not, you'll discover you haven't. A next action should be so clear and simple that it needs very little thinking or effort to complete.

For your brain, there's a big difference between "Math" and "Do math, chapter 7, exercise #1." One might feel overwhelming, while the other might seem ridiculously simple. However, in order to "do homework," you actually have to start by getting the book out of your backpack. Once you've done that, completing the math problem might be pretty easy. Stringing together a series of these simple actions results in the completion of "doing homework."

So how do you know if you have determined the very next action when going through this clarify step?

Here are a few helpful indicators:

- Does your next action include a *simple action verb*?
- Is it specific enough to know *where* it happens?
- Is it specific enough to describe any *tools* needed?
- Is it easily started without any further thought or decision-making?

If there's a task that you're having trouble getting started on, consider that you might have yet to identify the single next action. When you have it, try just taking that one single action, and then figure out the next one. Everything you will ever do will naturally follow this process. Actions generate movement, and movement creates momentum.

Never confuse motion with action.   —BENJAMIN FRANKLIN

The goal when thinking about action is to create *momentum* instead of worrying about success or completion. Success or completion comes as a *result* of enough momentum.

Take a look at the following chart, which shows a traditional to-do list vs. a true **next action list**. Each line represents a different way of thinking about the same task. What do you notice about it?

TO DO LIST	ACTION LIST
Homework	Complete review questions on p.28
College	Download Georgetown application
Mom	Order mom's birthday present on Amazon
Room	Pickup dirty clothes
Latrelle	Purchase "get well" card for Latrelle

Look carefully at both sides and ask yourself, "How *difficult* would it be to do the things on each of these lists?" Which list would make it easier to generate momentum? The specificity of the action list makes taking action easy and clear.

The Two-Minute Rule

Once a single next action is crystal clear, the next subquestion in the thinking process is to consider whether you can take action *immediately*. If the action is simple and won't take very long, the best thing to do is to take care of it right away. The quickest way to close any open loop is immediate completion. The Two-Minute Rule states that if you can complete an action in less than two minutes, do it right away. Get it off your plate, close the loop, and get it off your mind!

Two-minute items could be quick actions like handing in a homework assignment, putting dirty clothes in a hamper, giving Mom a permission slip, responding to a text, etc. If not completed right away, two-minute items can quickly build up a backlog and bog you down. Completing two-minute items is an easy way to quickly reduce volume and create some clear space—they are quick wins. If you *can't* complete an action in two minutes, then you'll have to track it for a later time.

2-MINUTE RULE

IF IT TAKES LESS THAN 2 MINUTES, JUST DO IT.

Map It for Later

Because most next actions can't be completed in under two minutes, they end up falling into a category of *next* but also *not right now*. We call this *deferred* action. Deferring until later means that you intend to do the action but recognize you can't take care of it immediately.

While successfully dealing with two-minute items can be helpful in keeping you moving through the day, it's what you do in the deferring process that will make the biggest difference.

Remember when we said that the clarify phase is the potential game changer? Buckle up, because the last few parts of the thinking process are potentially life-altering.

When you start to make things happen, you really begin to believe that you can make things happen. And that makes things happen.

—DAVID ALLEN

Are You Done?

For actions that can't be completed quickly, there is one final subquestion for consideration.

The first you've already answered: What is the very next visible action to take to make progress on this item? (What does "doing" look like?)

The last subquestion is: Will I be done after taking that action? If not, when will I be truly finished? (What will "done" look like?)

The first question helps you determine a *single action* to get you started, while the second will help you identify when to *stop* taking action. To know when to stop, all you need is a clear picture of what you want to accomplish when you're finished.

Clarifying both the very next action to take and determining what a finished outcome looks like are a powerful process and the most important part of this book. Because these two questions represent the keys to both control and perspective, let's look deeper at what we mean by a finished outcome and how we determine what "done" looks like.

ACTIONABLE CATEGORY #2: PROJECT

Determining what "doing" (next action) looks like is a critical piece of moving on anything. The close partner of determining what "doing" looks like is knowing what "done" (outcome) looks like. These outcomes are called **projects**.

Project: Any outcome that is going to take more than one action or session to complete.

PROJECT

A Project Is a Description of a Successful Outcome

An **outcome** is a description of what you want to be true when you are finished. "Finished" describes the point at which actions will no longer need to be tracked. It is what *successful* completion will look like. It is like crossing the finish line at the end of a race—once you've done that, the race is over for you.

Some examples of **projects**:

- Turn in finished book report.
- Complete preparation for science test.
- Get driver's license.
- Fill out Georgetown college application.

Notice how these projects describe a state of completion. If the project description is completed, then there aren't any more actions to take.

If you are clear on where you are going (outcome) *and* have a concrete next step (next action) to get there, you have what is necessary for both control and perspective, and you are set up for success. You are ready.

Projects You Create vs. Projects Assigned to You

Being a student means that you have teachers who will assign work to you. When they assign what they call "projects," the process for clarifying still applies. Such projects might be clarified to look something like this:

—Deliver speech on environmental change.

—Complete service project for social studies.

Likewise, you may also have projects assigned to you by a parent:

—Clean out garage.

—Clean room.

Other projects might be those you generate for yourself:

—Clean out car.

—Throw party for Caitlin.

—Create a working robot to clean my room for me.

Regardless of who *generates* the project, *you* are the one in control of clarifying it and deciding what a *successful* completion will look like.

The Transformative Process

Once you're able to transform all actionable stuff, you'll never look at it in the same way again. All actionable stuff will begin to represent opportunities for outcomes and actions.

If stuff is handled through the *fundamental thinking process*, it is always possible to achieve, maintain, or regain control. This might sound too good to be true. It might sound similar to clichés like, "You can do anything you set your mind to!" Let's get more specific and dig into this transformative process so it moves beyond theory and into practice.

Learning to Create the Conditions

The idea of transforming actionable stuff into outcomes and actions is both a simple concept and a subtle art form. At the beginning of this book we stated that while you are *not* in control of all the stuff that enters your world, you *are* in control of how to engage with it. You are in control of the process of transforming stuff into actions and outcomes and giving yourself the power and agility to act upon them.

Remember: You aren't in control of how much homework your teacher assigns, but you *are* in control how you handle the homework. You aren't in control of whom the coaches pick during tryouts, but you *are* in control of your preparation for tryouts. You aren't in control of how friends react to the things you share, but you *are* in control of the way you treat people and how you share your life with others. You aren't in control of what grade you get on a final, but you *are* in control how well prepared you are for the test.

When defining outcomes, the key is to focus on the things over which you *do* have control. If you have identified an outcome that is within your operational control, then success is very much up to *you*. We call this process *creating the conditions*. You can create conditions for things to happen, even if you don't have complete control over the results. For example, you can create the conditions for your best performance in a tryout, to be prepared for a test, or for a fun night with friends.

If, however, you base your success on external factors that are outside your operational control, you'll constantly face disappointment. Examples of external factors might include making people happy, getting first place, or having people like you.

Learning to base outcomes on what is *within* your operational control sets you up to win, no matter what.

In more practical terms, what does this transformation and this operational control look like? Here are some examples. Notice the subtle difference?

OUTSIDE OF CONTROL	WITHIN CONTROL
Make the varsity team.	Be at my best for tryouts.
Get an "A" in algebra.	Prepare for the algebra test.
Get more friends.	Pursue new relationships.
Go to Georgetown.	Submit application for Georgetown.

The outcomes on the left side are dependent on *external* factors (a coach, a teacher, peers, a college acceptance board). The outcomes on the right are dependent on no one but you. While the outcomes on the right don't guarantee the results on the left, they represent the conditions that you can create to make them happen. That's *true* control!

Walk Through It

The clarifying step will assign all stuff into one of six categories: **actions**, **projects**, **checklists**, **someday/maybes**, **reference**, or **trash**.

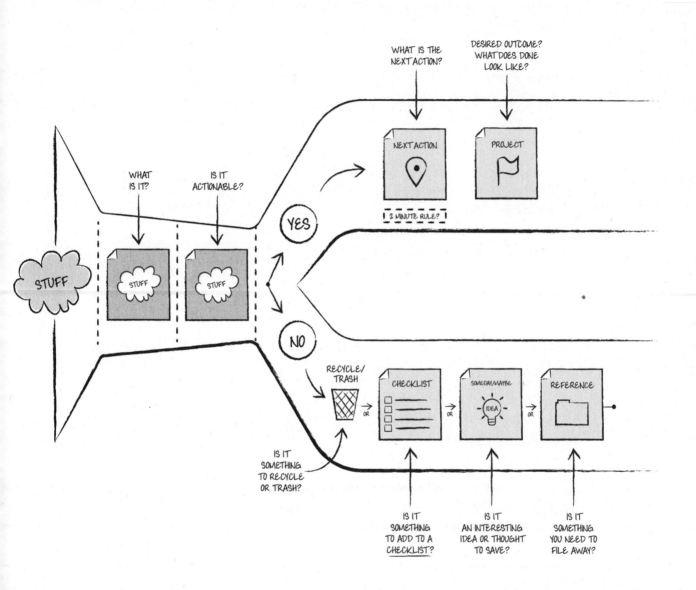

WHAT IS THE NEXT ACTION?

DESIRED OUTCOME? WHAT DOES DONE LOOK LIKE?

WHAT IS IT?

IS IT ACTIONABLE?

NEXT ACTION

PROJECT

2 MINUTE RULE?

STUFF

STUFF

STUFF

YES

NO

RECYCLE/ TRASH

CHECKLIST

SOMEDAY/MAYBE

IDEA

REFERENCE

OR

OR

OR

IS IT SOMETHING TO RECYCLE OR TRASH?

IS IT SOMETHING TO ADD TO A CHECKLIST?

IS IT AN INTERESTING IDEA OR THOUGHT TO SAVE?

IS IT SOMETHING YOU NEED TO FILE AWAY?

Let's look again at the complete *fundamental thinking process* using the transformer tool and apply the process to real-life examples.

Stuff:	Email from teacher containing syllabus
Actionable?:	No
Needed later?:	Possibly, yes.
New status:	REFERENCE

Stuff:	Applying for driver's license
Actionable?:	Yes
When done?:	When I have my actual driver's license
What's next?:	Take my driver's ed classes
New status:	PROJECT: Get driver's license
	NEXT ACTION: Look up dates of driver's ed classes online

Stuff:	Issue of skateboarding magazine
Actionable?:	No
Needed later?:	Not really, I've read it
New status:	TRASH

Stuff:	Basketball tryouts
Actionable?:	Yes
When done?:	When tryouts are over
What's next?:	Practice
New status:	PROJECT: Prepare for basketball tryouts
	NEXT ACTION: Shoot 50 three-point shots at the park

Stuff:	Prom
Actionable?:	Yes
When done?:	When prom is over
What's next?:	Find a date
New status:	PROJECT: Create the conditions for a great prom experience
	NEXT ACTION: Text Julia's friend to see if she is going to prom with anyone

Stuff:	New Avengers movie
Actionable?:	Not really. I want to see it, but I don't have to.
New status:	SOMEDAY/MAYBE

How Often to Clarify?

The clarify step requires thinking and decision-making. We recommend clarifying the stuff you've captured in buckets every twenty-four to forty-eight hours. Remember: After you clarify all your stuff for the first time and eliminate backlog, there won't be nearly as much stuff to assign to your buckets.

In order to successfully clarify your stuff on this schedule, you'll need to dedicate time to engage in the *fundamental thinking process*. This might work best for you early in the morning before class, right after school, or in the evenings. It might be most effective in a quiet library or in the noise of a coffee shop.

Because it takes valuable time and energy to complete this process, you shouldn't spend them doing it more than you need to. As you become an expert on step 2, the process becomes almost second nature, and it will take less time.

Some tips as you get started:

- When are you most fresh to think? In the a.m. or p.m.?
- Do you have any blocks of time in your week that already exist that might work for this process? Homeroom? A study hall? A quiet evening?

The results of your decision-making mean your stuff is no longer stuff, because it is now transformed. It is time to preserve these valuable decisions, keep them from going back into "in," and save all your valuable thinking and decision-making.

It's time for step 3 of the Five Steps: organize.

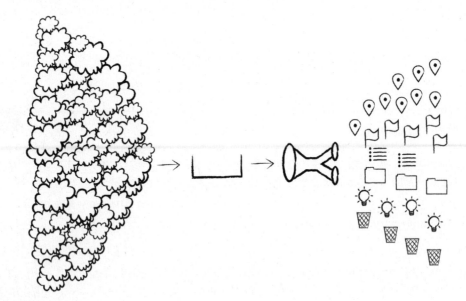

SUMMARY

Every item of stuff that has been captured requires a decision in order to transform it into a more useful form. The **transforming tool** is a visual guide to the *fundamental thinking* *process*. This process begins with the question "What is it?" Understanding if each item is actionable or nonactionable then divides up all your stuff into two categories.

Actionable items will require a **next action** and a finished **outcome**. Nonactionable items have to be categorized and ready to file for later as **trash**, a **checklist**, **someday/maybe**, or **reference**.

The clarifying process represents the most impactful of all **Five Steps**.

KEY TERMS

- Trash
- Reference
- Someday/Maybe

- Next Action
- Outcome
- Calendar

QUESTIONS FOR THOUGHT OR DISCUSSION

- Why do you think such an emphasis is put on the clarifying phase?
- Why do you think so few people take the time and energy to do the thinking required in this stage?
- What are the possible benefits of skipping this clarifying step? What are the possible consequences?
- Take a single item of stuff in your world. Ask yourself the question "What is it?" using the transformer tool map to guide you. Can you arrive at a clear answer?

STEP 3: ORGANIZE

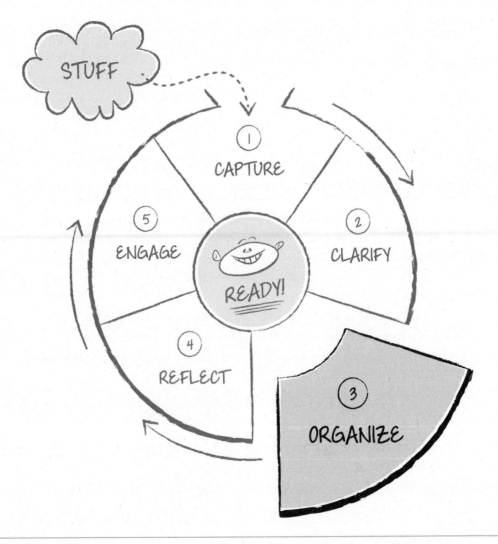

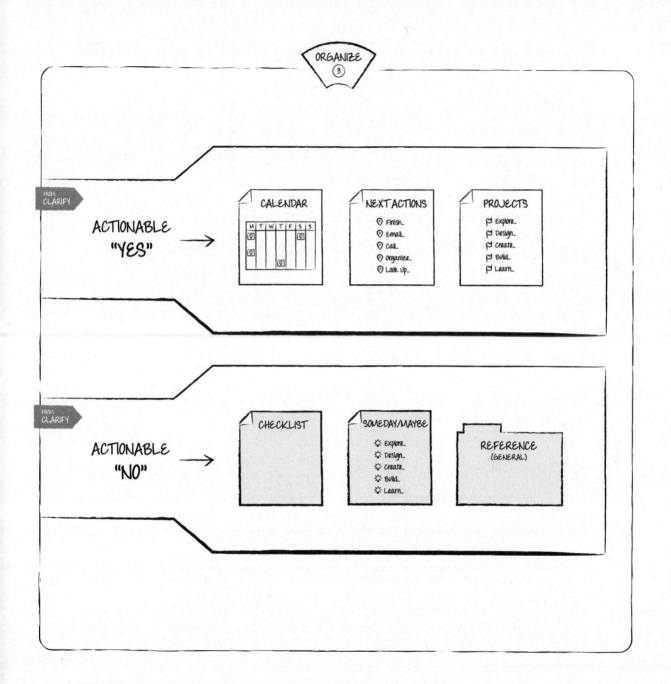

HOW DO I KEEP TRACK OF ALL THE THINGS I'VE CLARIFIED?

In step 2 you completed the *fundamental thinking process* called **clarify**. Stuff was transformed into one of six new forms, and everything is now in the form of actionable or nonactionable items. In other words, stuff is no longer just random items in your life.

In order to both preserve this thinking and take advantage of the **capturing** and **clarifying** work that you've done, you will need to hit "save" and preserve the results. To do so, step 3 involves parking everything in places where it can be easily accessed later, when it's convenient to do so. This is next step: **organize**.

In the Five Steps, "organize" does not mean making things pretty, pristine, aligned, and perfect.

Organize only involves putting items in places that match their meaning. These places will be intuitive and can be quickly accessed later with very little mental or physical effort. Organize is about providing yourself the best chance to continue moving forward with the least amount of resistance.

Organize: To physically, visually, or digitally sort and place items of similar meaning into discrete categories and locations.

Organization Tools

When people haven't made decisions on where to place things, their most common response seems to be putting them in wherever space is available. This behavior helps explain why backpacks, lockers, desks, counters, benches, and other spaces tend to gather piles of mail, notes, magazines. Even if this storing is done neatly, it won't result in being organized, at least not in the way we are describing. Having tidy piles of stuff will still require searching for and clarifying things all over again.

Therefore, before you're ready to organize the decisions you've made in step 2, you'll need to set up a few **organization tools**. Once these are in place, you'll be what's called **organize**

ready. In order to track your actionable and nonactionable items and become organize ready, you'll want to create a few simple lists and folders. For your actionable items, you'll need three primary lists. For your nonactionable items, you'll need two lists and some folders.

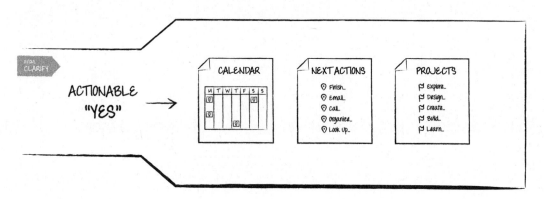

THE THREE ACTION LISTS

Let's start by creating the three lists you'll need for actionable items. We'll sometimes refer to these lists as maps, because they serve as dynamic guides that will help keep you on track of what you've decided is important to you. ("List" describes their *form*, while "map" describes their *function*.) The purpose of these maps is to preserve actionable decisions from step 2. Creating and learning to appropriately access them can help you achieve greater control and clarity and generate extra time, space, and energy for other things. Most of the stuff that was transformed in the clarify step will be tracked on these maps.

These three maps are:

- Calendar   • Next Action List   • Projects List

CALENDAR

M	T	W	T	F	S	S

NEXT ACTIONS

- ⚲ Finish...
- ⚲ Email...
- ⚲ Call...
- ⚲ Organize...
- ⚲ Look up...

PROJECTS

- ⚑ Explore...
- ⚑ Design...
- ⚑ Create...
- ⚑ Build...
- ⚑ Learn...

As a starting point for creating your maps, three sheets of lined paper or a simple Google Doc will be fine. Some people find that the list manager that comes preloaded on their phone (Reminders, Tasks, etc.) also works well. You can experiment with the particular form of your own maps until you find one that is simple and easy for you to use.

Let's look more specifically at these maps to determine which content to preserve on each.

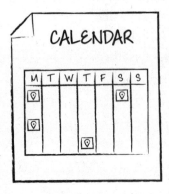

Calendar

For most people, the calendar is the most familiar of the maps. It's the first place you'll look each day to see what actions you've committed to.

A calendar should include a simple template that displays months of the year and days of the week. This map serves as the "hard landscape" and will store information about the places you need to be and when to be there, about the things you need to do at specific times, and about things that are happening on specific days.

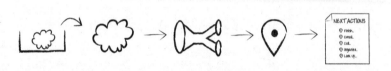

The calendar holds only three types of information:

1. Time-specific actions (soccer game, band concert, movie time, orthodontist appointment, etc.)

2. Day-specific actions (turn-in dates, concert ticket sales, etc.)

3. Day-specific reference items (birthdays, holidays, etc.)

Next Action

The **next action list** is a complete list of actions that *do not* need to happen at a specific time or in a specific location. Actions on this list take the form of the single next steps to move on anything that you decided needs your attention.

NEXT ACTIONS

◦ Finish...

◦ Email...

◦ Call...

◦ Organize...

◦ Look Up...

This is the list that will be most effective in supporting you to keep things moving in the right direction. It is a collection of descriptions of what "doing" looks like, so keep it as simple and as clear as possible.

Examples of actions will include errands to run, assignments to complete, messages to send, and activities to sign up for. While the actions on this list certainly may involve some self-discipline and effort, they should not require multiple steps or demand any additional decision-making. If they do, you may need to revisit the clarify step and determine the single best next action.

This list will likely be the largest of your maps. It will contain an extensive bank of actions that together hold the potential to create real momentum. It's also the most dynamic list, as it will potentially change quite a bit from day to day, expanding and contracting as you engage with it.

Deciding whether a clarified action should go on your calendar or next action list depends specifically on if the action is *time or date* specific.

EXAMPLES:

- You have a potluck to attend on Saturday. Assign it to your calendar: "Potluck at School, Saturday at 6:00 p.m."
- You have to buy food for the potluck. Place in your next action list: "Buy dessert with Mom for potluck dinner."
- You have a soccer tournament in a few weeks. Mark it on your calendar: "Soccer tournament, July 8, 9:00 a.m., field #6"
- You need your parents to fill out a school form. Add it to your next action list: "Have Dad sign my field trip form."
- Your band director tells you what time to arrive for a concert. Record it on your calendar: "Band concert, 6:45 p.m. arrival, 7:00 p.m. concert"
- One of your parents asked you to do a chore. Place it on the next action list: "Pick up dog poop in the yard."
- Concert tickets for your favorite band go on sale on a certain day at a certain time, and you want to get good seats. Remind yourself of the date on your calendar: "Buy tickets for [insert favorite band]"
- Meeting friends at a particular theater at a particular time to see a particular movie? Calendar.
- Dinner event? Calendar.
- Field trip for school? Calendar.

Projects

The **projects list** doesn't contain any next actions or calendar items. Instead, it will help keep you on course by containing all the outcomes, or what "done" looks like, on anything you have committed to doing that requires more than one action step or more than one session to complete. Projects will include things like larger school assignments to complete, creative ideas to explore, opportunities to pursue. You will access this list when you need to ensure that you are making visible progress and can revisit it to ensure that you have at least one next action for each of your projects. This list doesn't change nearly as often as the next action list, and as a result, you will tend to look at it less often.

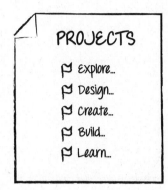

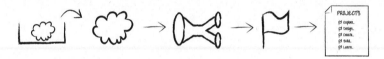

Organizing Nonactionable Items

Let's now turn our attention to organizing the nonactionable results we obtained in step 2. For these items, the tools to set up are two types of lists and a few folders.

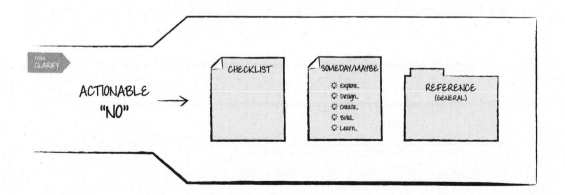

SOMEDAY/MAYBE

The someday/maybe list contains items that you decided you *might* want to do when the opportunity presents itself.

Generally speaking, cluster this list by topics: movies to see, trips to take, friends to get to know, books to read, websites to check out, etc. You need to consult this map only when you're looking for a creative spark or have generated some open time and clear space.

While this list holds great value, it doesn't require frequent viewing in order to stay in control and be successful. It is perfectly fine to procrastinate on the items it contains. Your someday/maybe items will be accessible when *you* are ready and eager to engage with them. As you gain more and more control, this list will present more and more opportunities.

CHECKLISTS

Routines and procedures that you've decided aren't yet habits take the form of checklists.

Unlike other lists, *how* you organize a checklist depends on its *content*.

The most important benefit of a checklist is having access to it *when* you need it. For example, if you play football and you want to make sure you have all your equipment before heading off to practice, a checklist might be very helpful. A quick scan will ensure that you haven't forgotten anything and are ready for a good practice. The basic recommendation for the best place to keep such a checklist would be wherever you would most likely see it before leaving for practice. This might be a tag attached to your bag or hanging by the front door.

The basic principle is to organize your checklists in places where you'd use them. Take a look at these samples. Where would you recommend putting them so that they would be most accessible when needed?

LIST	LOCATION
Packing checklist	_____
Before I Go to School checklist	_____
Workout checklist	_____

REFERENCE FILE

Nonactionable items that you decided you need to keep but don't require any action are reference.

While reference material is quite common and is easily identified ("I'm going to need that!"), for the sake of speed, people often put reference items back into their buckets or back into an "in" area for the purpose of finding them later (e.g., keeping email in an inbox). If you haven't designated a particular container to hold these items, somewhere like an inbox does become the safest and most convenient place to store them. The problem is that this can result in inboxes full of hundreds, even thousands of emails, or binders or backpacks overflowing with papers. While this does indeed keep reference material from being "lost," it doesn't make for quick or easy retrieval, and it can actually lead to more work and more mental effort and energy to manage, which defeats the whole purpose of organizing.

If you leave things in "in," such as an email, then every time you open up your email and do a quick scan, you'll have to do a small amount *re*-decision-making. Your brain has to reengage and say, "Okay . . . that's info for this, this is for that, etc." Even if you think the process doesn't take very long, those hundreds or even thousands of emails that you have already made a decision about can continue to hold some part of your attention, which is an unnecessary use of valuable cognitive energy.

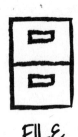

FILE

A more efficient practice is to proactively make a few decisions as to where you are going to keep your physical/analog and digital reference materials, and then set up **reference files** to hold them. Once you have created these reference files, you can just deposit reference items as soon as they show up in the clarify process in the appropriate place. When you need to access them, your brain will know exactly where to look. This is organization at its finest: easy file, easy retrieval, minimum effort. Being organized is like offering a treat for your brain.

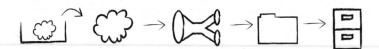

To set up a *paper* and *physical* reference file, most people find they need only a single file drawer or bin that can hold folders. For organizing *digital* files, there are a number of services that provide storage for all forms of content. Digital reference files can be stored using Google Drive, Apple's iCloud Drive, Dropbox, and many others.

WHEW!

Once you decide on the location—the *where* of your reference files—you can begin simply by placing material into folders and sorting them.

To be organize ready, it really doesn't matter *how* you organize your reference, as long as file and retrieval is quick and efficient. A neat and tidy system is not a requirement, so if your own way of doing things is more appealing, keep it. Just make sure your file retrieval is seamless and easy.

Organize Ready

If you already have organization tools in place for the actionable and nonactionable items that resulted from the clarify step, the *fundamental thinking process* can flow quickly and naturally without much thinking at all. You will have established an if/then procedure that will be easy to follow through on.

IF _____ [category], THEN ORGANIZE _____ [here].

For example, if I get reference material emailed to me, then I organize in Google Drive alphabetically.

Reaching this level of organize ready doesn't have to be an elaborate or complex process. It really is just a matter of preparing a few lists and file folders and, more important, making some decisions about *where* things will go. The system you're creating to manage your world *only* needs to be as complex as you need it to be to be in control. Don't make it harder or more complicated than necessary.

So, pause for a moment and reflect: Are you currently capture ready? Are you currently organize ready? What tools might you need to add to your system to be both capture ready and organize ready?

Workstations

One additional tool that can help you become organize ready is a workstation. A workstation is any location where you have access to everything you need to effectively execute steps 1 through 3.

Pilots have a cockpit; professional athletes have a training room or practice facility; office workers have their cubicle. What about you? Do you have a place that allows you to access *what* you need, *when* you need it, with little resistance, and inspires you to do the best work possible? Having a workstation can be a huge boost toward control and creativity.

Workstations can come in many forms: a desk in a bedroom, a corner in the kitchen, even a mobile workstation in a backpack so you can be ready no matter where you are. The key is to be able to quickly be at your best without much effort. A workstation is a space that looks in a way, feels in a way, and is equipped in a way that brings the best out of you. This workstation should have all the tools necessary for you to be both capture ready and organize ready.

To create or enhance your current workstation, think about what you still might need in order to be successful (a bucket, charging cords, pens/pencils, paper, mobile devices, jump drives, files/books, etc.). Spend some time carefully setting up this space and give yourself a boost toward being organize ready.

Ready . . . Set . . . Map Check?

So far we've examined the process of corralling and capturing a wide range of stuff using buckets and capture tools, in order to gain control and quiet the mind.

We've described how to make clarifying decisions about each item of stuff through the *fundamental thinking process* visualized in the transformer tool, and then we transformed it all into more usable forms of actions, projects, checklists, someday/maybe, reference, and trash.

We've explained how to preserve those decisions on maps that will guide you along the way or file them into a reference system that allows for quick file and retrieval.

If you've done these things, you're set up to be in control for success. You can now start aggressively moving forward and making things happen. In order to feel comfortable and confident in this progress, it's important to know you are heading not just in *any* direction but in the *right* direction. Keep in mind the pitfalls that are still lurking.

You will still have to make sure you apply your attention to *the right things*. That's *true* control. To do this, pause and do a **map check**.

This is where you slow down to speed up.

Welcome to step 4: reflect.

SUMMARY

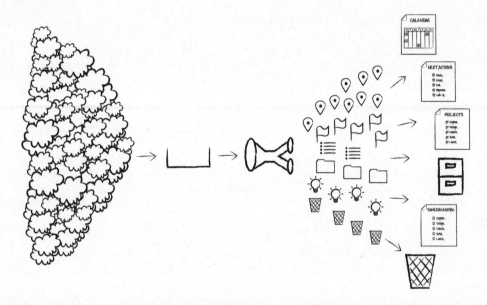

Once decisions are made in the clarify process, don't waste any time making those decisions again. Parking the results of decisions maximizes effectiveness with the least amount of effort. There are a few maps that are used to hold the results of decisions and keep you on track. The calendar keeps track of date- and time-specific actions. The next action list keeps an inventory of all the visible next actions. The projects list keeps an inventory of larger outcomes to track. The someday/maybe list keeps a bank of ideas to explore when control is achieved. Checklists help establish new habits. Reference material is filed so that it can be easily retrieved.

KEY TERMS

- Organize
- Organize Tools
- Next Action List
- Calendar
- Projects List
- Someday/Maybe List
- Reference File
- Checklist
- Organize Ready

QUESTIONS FOR THOUGHT OR DISCUSSION

- How would you describe the difference between "neat" and "organized"?
- How would you describe the form and function of each of the different maps? Do you have any form of the maps in place already?
- What tools do you still need in order to be organize ready?
- Do you have a workstation? If not, is there a location that makes sense for you? If you have one, what could you do to make it more effective?

STEP 4: REFLECT

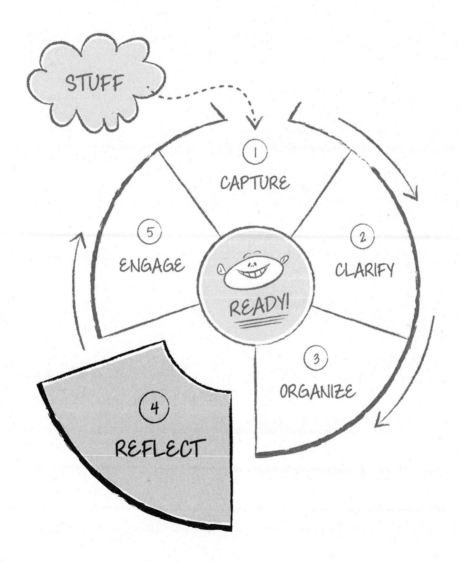

REFLECT
(4)

DAILY REVIEW

1. CHECK YOUR CALENDAR
2. CHECK YOUR NEXT ACTION LIST
3. CHECK RELEVANT CHECKLISTS

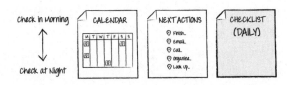

Check in Morning ↕ Check at Night

CALENDAR | NEXT ACTIONS | CHECKLIST (DAILY)

WEEKLY REVIEW

GET CLEAR

1. Collect loose papers and materials.
2. Do a mindsweep to empty your head.
3. Get "in" to empty.

Get CLEAR

① COLLECT LOOSE PAPERS ② MIND SWEEP ③ GET "IN" TO EMPTY

GET CURRENT

4. Review previous calendar entries.
5. Review upcoming calendar entries.
6. Review next action list.
7. Review project list.
8. Review any relevant checklists.

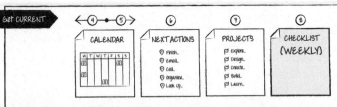

Get CURRENT

← ④ ― ⑤ → ⑥ ⑦ ⑧

CALENDAR | NEXT ACTIONS | PROJECTS | CHECKLIST (WEEKLY)

GET CREATIVE

9. Review someday/maybe list.
10. Be creative and courageous!

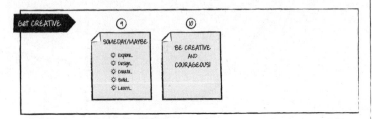

Get CREATIVE

⑨ SOMEDAY/MAYBE ⑩ BE CREATIVE AND COURAGEOUS!

REFLECT ON WHAT? WHEN?

The reflect step is like a pause button for life. It is a review of what's happening in your current reality and of your future intentions, and then an update of the choices you've made.

The capture, clarify, and organize steps essentially involve your writing information into your system. In that sense, you are the "writer" of your story. The reflect step involves your taking a step back and becoming the "editor" of your story. The combination of your system and step 4 will help you refine the life story you've been imagining.

Reflect: To review and update the contents of your maps to bring them up-to-date with your current reality, so that you can make informed and effective choices.

While steps 1 through 3 can help you *achieve* or *regain* control, it's step 4 that helps you *maintain* it. It enhances the control you've achieved with some higher levels of **perspective**. It's where the "what" you are doing and the "why" you're doing it come together. Week after week, this step will help you clear your head, keep your system current, stoke your creative energy, and build your courage.

The 3-D Glasses

Up to this point you've invested time, focus, and energy into making decisions and mapping the results of those decisions. The maps you've created serve as guides to getting results, gaining control, and making things happen.

But *how often* should you look at your maps? *Which ones* should you look at? *When* should you look at them?

In real life, 3-D glasses enable you to watch movies or see things with a greater sense of depth and perspective. Think of "reflect" as putting on a special pair of 3-D glasses. Using the maps you've created, these glasses serve as a metaphor for three *different* levels of reviews (3 depths = 3-D).

3 D GLASSES

Each one helps you see what you need to at the appropriate time:

1. Daily review (What do I need to do?)
2. Weekly review (Am I clear? Am I current? Am I creative?)
3. Levels of Focus review (Where am I going? Why?)

In step 4 we'll focus on the first two depths—the daily review and the weekly review. In the next part of the book we'll explore the third depth—the Levels of Focus.

I know where I'm going and I know the truth,
and I don't have to be what you want me to be.
I'm free to be what I want.

—MUHAMMAD ALI

Daily Reviews

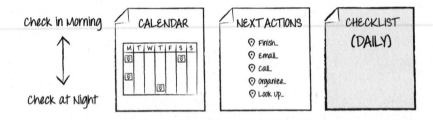

The daily review is the first depth in the 3-D review. Its purpose is to help you understand what you need to do *today*.

To determine that, use the two lists that hold all your actions: your calendar and your next action list. At a minimum, try to look at these lists twice each day: first thing in the morning and before you go to bed. You may also find it helpful to include a review of any relevant checklists (e.g., Before I Leave the House for School checklist, My [Sport] checklist, My [Activity] checklist).

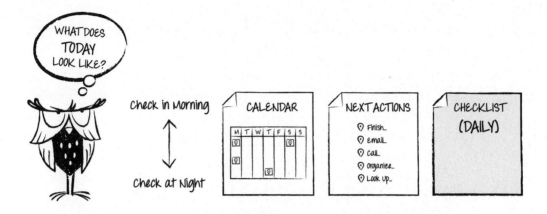

CALENDAR—Check this map as you begin each day to remind yourself where you need to be and when you need to be there. Depending on the number of items in your schedule, you may have to consult your calendar throughout the day.

NEXT ACTION LIST—Check this map each morning to help you make decisions about what or what not to do that day. Doing so doesn't mean that you *have* to do something written on it—quite the opposite. When you can scan this map and recognize that you are in good shape with your responsibilities, it allows your brain to let go, so that you can relax and engage with something you're passionate about without any guilt, reservation, or nagging. One of the hidden benefits of your maps is that you can decide *not* to engage with anything on them without experiencing worry or stress. Why? Because you can return to them and immediately know exactly what needs to be done. That's freedom.

CHECKLISTS—Look at your checklists at a time when and in a location where they'll be helpful. Each checklist serves a different purpose, so when and how often you check it will depend on the list's content. For example, you may have a checklist of items that you want to review before you leave the house for school. Another checklist may be hanging in your locker, containing items you want to review before you leave school for home.

Each daily review takes only a few seconds. The more you engage with it, the more you and your brain will learn to trust your calendar, next action list, and checklists as trusted parts of your system. The daily review brings a sense of short-term, day-to-day control. To *maintain* this control, it will be important to gain a more complete view of your world. The next depth of review to do is a weekly review.

A few seconds a day is usually all you need for review,
as long as you're looking at the right things at the right time.
—DAVID ALLEN

Weekly Reviews

The purpose of a weekly review is to help you maintain control by clearing your head, keeping your system current, and stoking your creative energy.

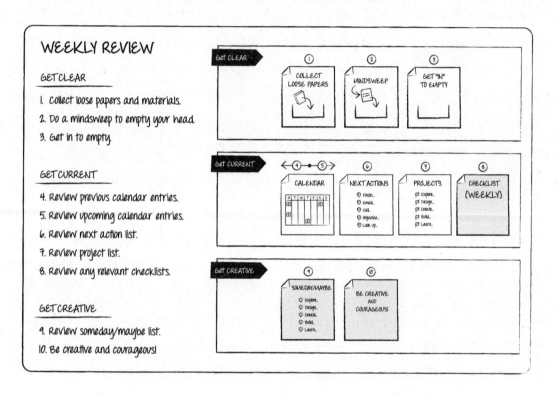

> The Weekly Review provides life's Stop, Look, and Listen sign. It aligns your actions to your thinking as you think about your actions.
>
> —DAVID ALLEN

PART 1: GET CLEAR

This review helps you gather up any stuff that may have accumulated over the past week. It includes *physical* stuff, *digital* stuff, and the subtler *mental* stuff that may be rattling around in your head.

TO GET CLEAR

Collect loose papers and materials—Identify any residue from the past week by doing a stuff hunt. Look for the stuff in your world that is not REDS (reference, equipment, decoration, supplies). For example, you might dump out the contents of your backpack and repack it: old sandwich (REDS = no, put in bucket), form for parents to sign (REDS = no, put in bucket), dirty gym clothes (REDS = no, put in bucket), books (REDS = yes, back in backpack), pencils and pens (REDS = yes, back in backpack), notebook (REDS = yes, back in backpack).

Mind sweep—Using a mind sweep, empty your head to capture anything that's on your mind. Place the results of your mind sweep in your bucket.

Get "in" to empty—Empty your buckets using the clarify and organize steps. For example: old sandwich (Actionable = no, Trash), form for parents to sign (Actionable = yes, put in Mom's "in" box, two-minute rule), dirty gym clothes (Actionable = yes, put in laundry basket, two-minute rule), and clear each item on your mind sweep list.

Upon completion of this part of the review, you are once again clear. Everything that could potentially need your attention is once again corralled and captured.

Getting current helps ensure that the maps you are relying on are complete and accurate. It involves removing outdated reminders and adding any new information. At the end of this part of the weekly review you can confidently say to yourself, your parents, or your teachers, "I am current. I know what 'doing' looks like [calendar, next actions]. I know what 'done' looks like [projects]."

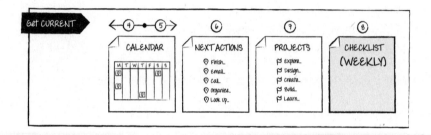

TO GET CURRENT

Review previous calendar entries—Look back through the past few weeks of your calendar. Do you see any reminders of something you need to do? You might realize, "I had my birthday party last week. Oh, yeah, I need to write thank-you notes." Put that on your next action list.

Review upcoming calendar entries—Look at your upcoming week, and then several weeks after that. Capture any actions about projects or actions required for upcoming events. For example, if you see that you have a school field trip in two weeks, you'll be reminded that you need to hand in your permission form. Or you may see you that your friend's birthday party is soon and you still need to get a gift. Capture both on your next action list.

Review next action list—Look at your next action list and start by marking off actions that you have completed. Next, add any new actions.

Review projects list—Check your projects list and make sure you have at least one next action associated with every project. For example: You see you have a book report due for English in two weeks and do not have a next action identified. You might capture, "Get *To Kill a Mockingbird* from the library." Now this project is up-to-date and has a current next action.

Review any relevant checklists—Like your daily review checklists, there may be lists or checklists you'd like to assess on a weekly basis. For example, you may want to review:

- Your sports or activities calendars
- A list of your favorite quotes for weekly inspiration
- A list of questions you'd like to ask yourself

Consider if there a list or checklist that you'd benefit from reviewing weekly.

PART 3: GET CREATIVE

GTD is not simply a method for making lists and keeping them current. While these are critical components of using a trusted system, ultimately, your system can lead you to new levels of clear space and possibilities. The Get Creative step is all about exploring the boundaries of your creativity and courage.

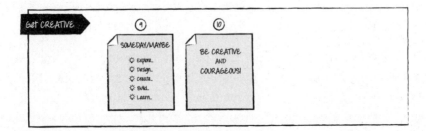

TO GET CREATIVE

Someday/Maybe—Look back at the ideas you've been capturing along the way and have put on your someday/maybe list. While it is freeing to capture ideas without having to do anything about them, it's a good practice to review these lists from time to time and ask yourself, "Is there anything on here that I want to take action on now?" If you answer yes to any item, move that item over to your projects list or next action list. This "activates" them and brings them into your daily reviews and weekly reviews and commits you to move on them and generate some action to create momentum.

For example, after seeing an inspiring movie a few years ago, you may have captured "Go to Paris." Recently, a sign at school announced a summer trip to Paris with scholarships available. You think to yourself, "Why not me? I'll move this into my system and see how far I can take this. What's the worst that can happen?"

Project: Look into school Paris trip.

Next action: Send email to trip contact to get information about the trip and scholarship.

Be Creative and Courageous!—Are there any other new wonderful, thought-provoking ideas you can capture and add to your system? This may be the perfect time—go for it!

Taking the time and energy to do reviews each day and each week will ensure you can *stay* ready. It will help you maintain a sense of control and confidence heading into each day and each week, knowing that you are ready for what lies ahead.

People often say that motivation doesn't last. Well, neither does bathing. That's why we recommend it daily.   —ZIG ZIGLAR

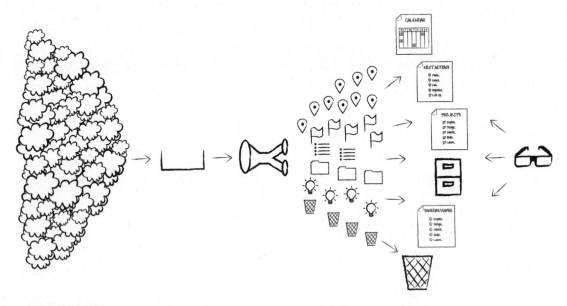

SUMMARY

The reflect step involves pausing to slow down and look back. It starts with capturing and clarifying any unprocessed stuff and conducting map checks to make sure that you are on track to make progress on decisions you've already made.

The frequency with which you check each map depends on both the type of map and the complexity of your current reality. The 3-D glasses are a metaphor for three different depths of reviews—the daily review, the weekly review, and Levels of Focus.

The weekly review is the core behavior in maintaining control, and it involves three steps—Getting Clear, Getting Current, and Getting Creative.

KEY TERMS

- Reflect
- Daily Review
- Weekly Review

QUESTIONS FOR THOUGHT OR DISCUSSION

- How often do you think you will need to check your maps to stay in control?
- Where would be the optimal location for you to do a weekly review? What is required of you in order to conduct a weekly review?
- What are the possible benefits of doing a weekly review on a consistent basis?

STEP 5: ENGAGE

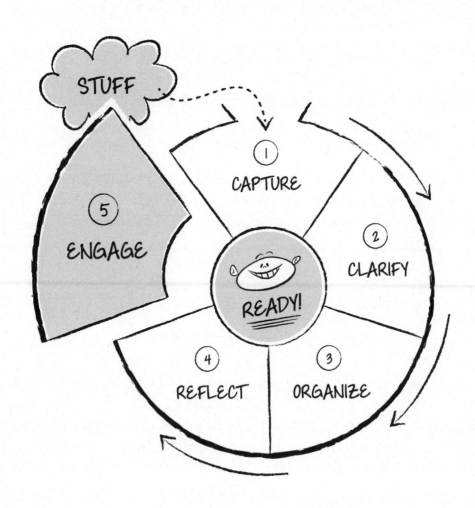

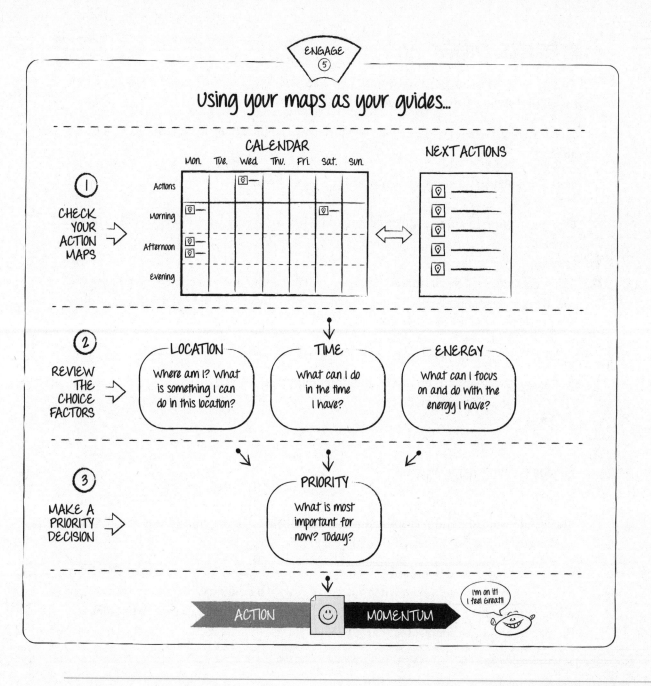

STEP FIVE: ENGAGE

This is it—the last of the Five Steps. The step where you get to take advantage of all the thinking you've already completed.

This is the step where, with the help of your maps and intuition, you choose an action and do it.

This is where you make progress toward the plans you've made.

Engage: To clearly, fully, and confidently do what you know you should be doing in the moment.

The tools and strategies in this step support you in making trusted choices about how you spend your time and energy. Using your next action lists will help you get things done with the *least* amount of effort possible.

> If you spend too much time thinking about a thing,
> you'll never get it done.
> —BRUCE LEE

Engage Is About Being Mindful

The goal of step 5 is to be appropriately engaged and present in every moment, including during times of fun and pleasure. It also means being able to engage in the not-so-fun moments that require some self-discipline and grit.

One of the underrated and perhaps unexpected benefits of GTD is the ability to remain calm, cool, and collected, even when your world gets a bit crazy. When you are not scrambling, panicking, or stressing, you have the opportunity and energy to actually focus on the people and the circumstances around you.

Additionally, because you have gained a sense of control and have assembled a complete inventory of what's happening in your world, you may often find that the best use of your time, focus, and energy is *not taking action*. This is called **clear space**, and it is becoming more and more rare in the age of connectivity.

Generating and discovering clear space gives you a newfound opportunity to:

- Chill out.
- Relax and listen to your favorite music.
- Be fully present for a friend.
- Strike up a conversation with someone new.
- Daydream about or pursue something you've captured on your someday/maybe list.

When you are no longer at the mercy of stuff coming at you, you have significantly more choices of what to do and when to do it. With such a large inventory of choices identified, though, a new question will often arise: How do I know what action to do and when to do it?

Let's take a look at this process of choosing an action and how you can confidently make choices that will help you move forward.

> Wherever you are, be all there.
>
> —JIM ELLIOT

Use Your Maps

To help you feel confident in how you spend your time, the first thing to do is a quick map check. A glance at your calendar and next action list can help ensure that you are where you need to be and that you have taken care of any pressing actions.

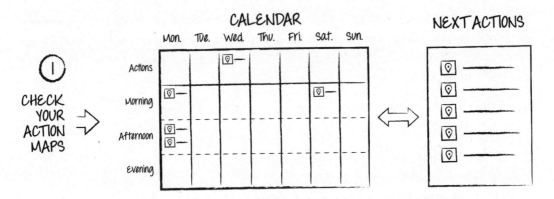

If there isn't anything urgent that needs to be done immediately, you'll have a decision to make among a lot of options. There's a tool that can help you choose to engage with the best possible one. Meet the spotlight.

The Four Criteria of the Spotlight

By the time you've entered middle school or high school, you have, whether you're aware of it or not, already established some habits, either good or bad, when it comes time to do what you need to do. Some people will tend to wait until the last minute, when the pressure is so high that they have no choice but to take action (e.g., staying up late or waking up extra early in the morning to finish schoolwork). Others will choose what to do based on whatever they are in the mood to do at that moment (e.g., selecting the easy assignment despite knowing the harder one is more important).

While these are common strategies, most are driven by emotional, social, or parental pressure. However, being common strategies does not necessarily make them the most *effective* strategies. Step 5 is intended to help equip you to be "uncommon"—to set you apart from the crowd and make you the most effective you can be.

An alternative strategy to doing what is most recent or most pressing (latest and loudest) is called the **spotlight strategy**. It uses the maps you've created to assist you in becoming more effective in your decision-making. The spotlight supports your brain in considering a unique mix of four criteria:

- Location
- Time
- Energy
- Priority

These criteria can support you in being calm and confident in the action choices you make. Let's take a look at each of them.

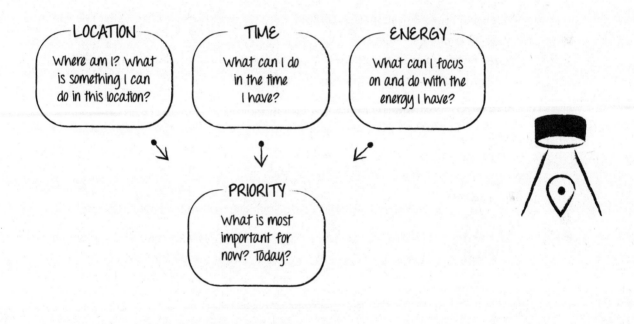

LOCATION
Where am I? What is something I can do in this location?

TIME
What can I do in the time I have?

ENERGY
What can I focus on and do with the energy I have?

PRIORITY
What is most important for now? Today?

I am rather like a mosquito in a nudist camp; I know what I want to do, but I don't know where to begin.   —STEPHEN BAYNE

TIME

A multimillion-dollar industry has arisen around the concept of "time management." In reality, though, you can't manage time. Time is moving whether you want it to or not. There will be times when the minutes and hours tend to move slow and others when they seem to fly by!

TIME
what can I do
in the time
I have?

You can, however, manage how you *engage* with time. Here are some questions that can guide you in engaging with it appropriately:

- How much time do you have available before your next scheduled activity? Five minutes? Ten minutes? Thirty minutes?
- Based on the answer to that question, what is something you could effectively engage with or accomplish in that amount of time?

If you have only five minutes available, beginning the thinking process for a big project might not be the best choice. For such a short window, you may have time for only a brief message, a quick scan of a website, or a fast unpack/repack of your backpack. These five-minute investments are *not* insignificant. As a matter of fact, taking full advantage of them can help you generate some clear space later.

If you have a thirty-minute window of time, then sending that short message or checking a website might not be the best option. In fact, they may actually represent a pitfall of distraction and result in procrastination.

A thirty-minute block might give you enough time to engage with a more sizable type of action. You likely have actions that require some extended thought, more materials, or a series of steps in order to gain momentum. Thirty minutes could represent a good block to do some brainstorming or extended reading or to clarify stuff that has gathered in your buckets.

Learning to recognize the different types of action that are best suited for various-size blocks of time can ensure that, given any-size window, you are ready to engage appropriately.

ENERGY

Energy comes in many forms—physical, mental, and emotional. You don't have to be at a level of full energy to feel continually ready and in control. You can even be tired and still effectively engage.

> ENERGY
> What can I focus on and do with the energy I have?

It can be helpful to have a basic understanding of your own energy levels and how they affect when you *think* best, *work* best, and *relax* best. This will enable you to not only match blocks of time but also your energy level to an appropriate action. How do you do that?

Here are some questions that can help:

- When are you at your best? In the early morning? Midday? Late at night?
- When do you feel the most awake and alert and have the most stamina to do challenging things?

Understanding when you are working at full capacity can guide you in deciding when to engage with the most challenging things that you have committed to do.

Do you have an action or project that you know will require some extra motivation on your part? If you put it off until the last minute, you could be stuck dealing with it when you are at your least effective. Instead, take on those challenging actions when you are at your peak performance.

On the flip side, when do you start to drag? When are you simply fried?

Understanding when these ebbs typically occur can help you recognize your own low-energy status, and you can learn when to take action on things that require very little focus. Low-energy times may present a good opportunity for sending a

quick message or cleaning a drawer while you watch a movie. If you've mapped actions really well, you can still find and take actions that can create some great momentum. This ready state just has a different capacity.

LOCATION

Location refers to the when and where you *can* actually engage. It means recognizing what you can realistically accomplish given your *location* and the *time of day*.

For example, you can't call to schedule a haircut at 10:00 p.m. if the barbershop is closed. You can't send an email if you're somewhere that lacks Wi-Fi or connectivity. You can't run an errand to a store that is too far to make a trip practical.

LOCATION
Where am I? What is something I can do in this location?

Rather than being blocked by all these potential "can't"s, using location means asking yourself, "Given the time of day, where I am, and the resources around me, what *can* I take action on?" The resulting answer might limit your options, but it'll assure that you engage appropriately.

PRIORITY

Of the four criteria of the spotlight, the last one, priority, will be the most influential.

PRIORITY
What is most important for now? Today?

Some things just have to get done *now*. If you have an assignment that is due in the morning, your energy, time, and location may have to take a back seat. Sometimes priority determines quite clearly and obviously what you need to engage in next.

WHAT NEEDS TO GET DONE?

If there is a test coming up an hour, studying might win out over your current energy and mood. If you have to have an urgent conversation with a friend, energy and time may not matter.

You can apply the spotlight criteria to your world whenever they'll be useful. Given the time of day, your location, your energy, and all that you have going on, what is the best thing for you to be doing *right now*?

Are you ready to continue reading, or is there something else pulling at your attention? If so, you know what to do!

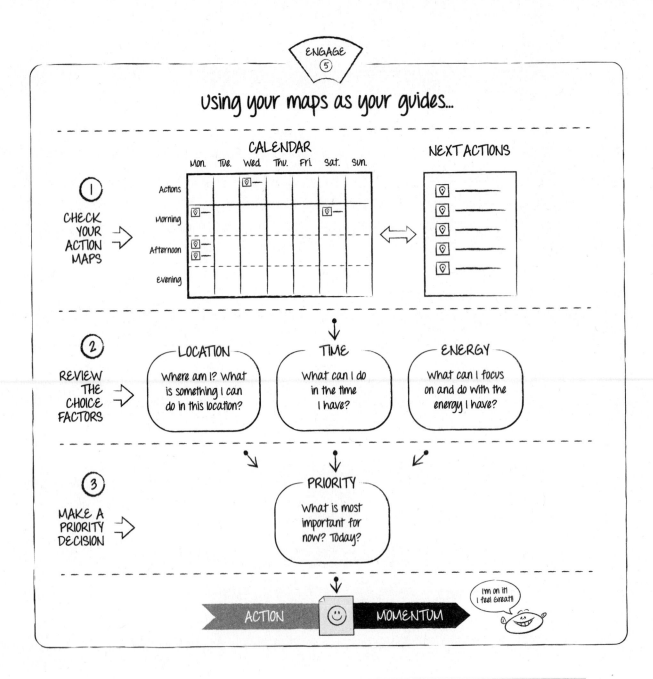

SUMMARY

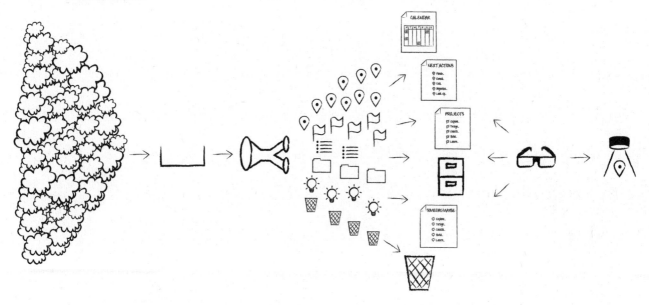

To engage means to make a decision about how best to interact with your current conditions. Making the best decision about what to do next can be supported by checking maps and having some decision-making criteria. The spotlight is a tool that provides four useful criteria.

KEY TERMS

• Engage   • Time   • Location   • Priority   • Energy

QUESTIONS FOR THOUGHT OR DISCUSSION

• When given a window of time—study hall, an evening after school, an open Saturday morning—how do you decide what to do? How certain do you feel you are making the best choice?

• How might you apply the four criteria of the spotlight to your studies or work?

GAINING PERSPECTIVE: LEVELS OF FOCUS

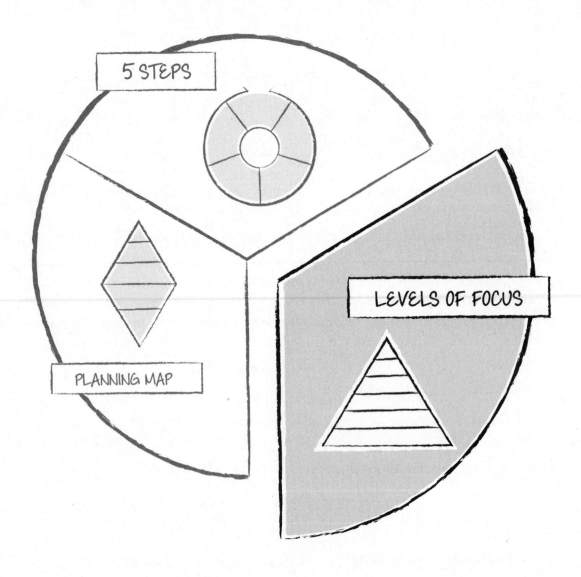

5 STEPS

PLANNING MAP

LEVELS OF FOCUS

In the previous section, we shared how, by using the Five Steps, you can get back to ready and experience the value of handling stuff. Now that you understand and know how to achieve control, let's move forward!

The purpose of getting control in the first place is to be clear of distractions so that you can focus. Now that you are ready, the question is: Where do you *put* your focus?

In this part of the book, we're going to explore perspective using the third and most dynamic depth of the 3-D model from step 4, the Levels of Focus.

Consider this: How do you tend to feel when others tell you what to do? Do you become annoyed or glad or frustrated or happy or creative—or perhaps a mix of all these? In contrast, how do you tend to feel when *you* are the one making decisions and choosing the ideas and doing the activities that are important to you? It likely feels quite a bit different.

In many ways, achieving independence and freedom is related to your ability to manage your focus—your ability to gain perspective. In this section, you'll have the opportunity to capture your thoughts and ideas on each of the Levels of Focus maps. The Levels of Focus will help you capture, clarify, and manage your focus and perspective *over time*. As you gain some new perspective by creating and updating your Levels of Focus, you'll likely start to see some new and exciting possibilities. Let's explore these levels in more detail.

LEVELS OF FOCUS

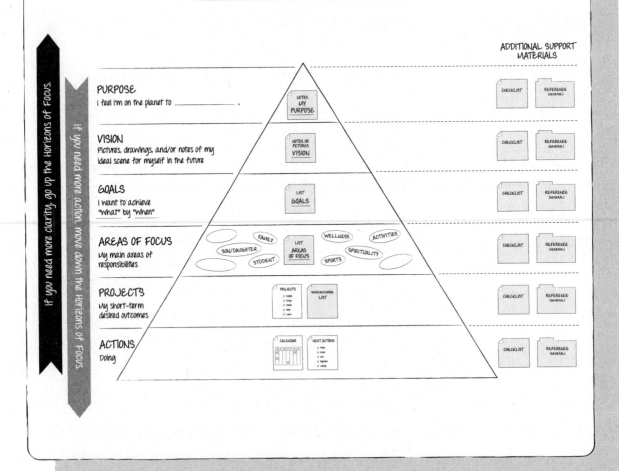

ADDITIONAL SUPPORT MATERIALS

If you need more clarity, go up the Horizons of Focus.

If you need more action, move down the Horizons of Focus.

PURPOSE
I feel I'm on the planet to _____ .

NOTES MY PURPOSE

CHECKLIST   REFERENCE (GENERAL)

VISION
Pictures, drawings, and/or notes of my ideal scene for myself in the future

NOTES OR PICTURES VISION

CHECKLIST   REFERENCE (GENERAL)

GOALS
I want to achieve "what" by "when"

LIST GOALS

CHECKLIST   REFERENCE (GENERAL)

AREAS OF FOCUS
My main areas of responsibilities

FAMILY SON/DAUGHTER STUDENT

LIST AREAS OF FOCUS

WELLNESS ACTIVITIES SPIRITUALITY SPORTS

CHECKLIST   REFERENCE (GENERAL)

PROJECTS
My short-term desired outcomes

PROJECTS   SOMEDAY/MAYBE LIST

CHECKLIST   REFERENCE (GENERAL)

ACTIONS
Doing

CALENDAR   NEXT ACTIONS

CHECKLIST   REFERENCE (GENERAL)

Zoom In, Zoom Out

The Levels of Focus can help you create, store, and retrieve information from different points of perspective. Like the mapping app on your phone, you can think of the Levels of Focus as a dynamic mapping app for life. If you need a broader overview of where life is heading, you zoom out to get a wider view. If you need to make something happen with more specific, action-oriented directions, you zoom in to get a more precise view.

Think about Google Maps. If you want to consider the Earth as a whole, you might zoom out to a view that shows the entire planet—a much higher perspective. Because you're not looking at the level of streets or homes, you might notice certain larger-scale details, which, in turn, might raise certain larger questions. What do you think about when looking at this view?

In contrast, let's say you are trying to find a field for a soccer game. In that case, you'd zoom in to a view of the map that includes turn-by-turn information from your home to the field. This represents a lower perspective—a much different view with a different purpose. Looking at this map you'll probably notice different details and ask different kinds of questions. What thoughts are triggered from this view?

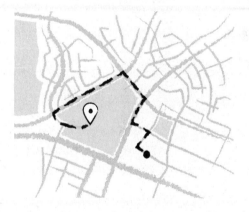

Moving up and down your life's Levels of Focus is something that you already do naturally. By learning more about the Levels of Focus tool, you can use this zoom in/zoom out type of thinking to support your journey of maintaining control and perspective.

The Purpose of the Levels

The Levels of Focus are part of the larger GTD system. They can hold information that can offer the right cues, to notice at the right time, about the things that are important to you. Imagine the Levels of Focus as the chapters of a book titled *The Story of My Life*. The information contained in them can help you navigate through adventures and challenges so that you can see *what* you are doing and how that connects to *why* you are doing it.

When you learn to capture ideas and organize them into their appropriate levels, you're effectively writing into a small piece of your story. In this sense, you have some operational control as the *author* of your story. When you learn to step back and review and reflect on the content at each of the levels, you'll begin to notice if something needs tweaking, deleting, or adjusting, and you can make the necessary change. In this sense, you also take on the role of *editor* in your life's story.

Over time, you'll have many opportunities to edit your story and make course corrections. And in the not-so-distant future, you'll begin to take on total freedom and responsibility for where you're headed. The Levels of Focus will support you in successfully navigating life with confidence.

Levels of Focus

There are six levels in this tool, each of which will help you see your life differently and determine where to put your focus and why. Let's look at these levels, pausing to capture your current thoughts and ideas on the appropriate map at each.

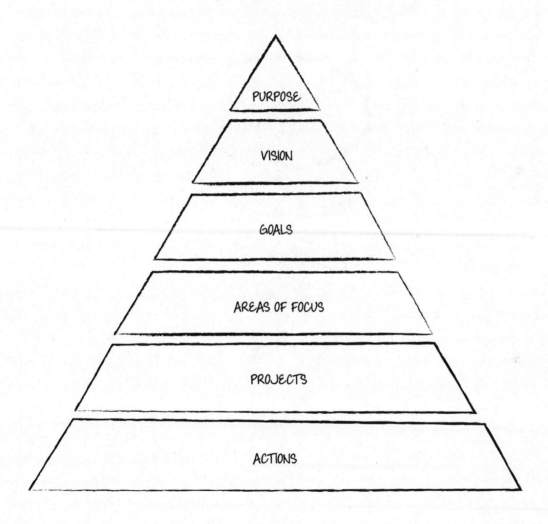

LEVELS OF FOCUS

PURPOSE

VISION

GOALS

AREAS OF FOCUS

PROJECTS

ACTIONS

PURPOSE

Purpose is the highest of all the levels. It holds the broadest view of your life, just like the zoomed-out image of the Earth in Google Maps. It begs the simple but significant question "Why?"

For example, "Why am I here? I feel I'm on the planet to _____."
Or, "Why am I here? I feel my purpose is to _____."

How would you answer this significant question as the person you are now? Using the Purpose map on the following page, take a moment to capture your initial thoughts on why you're here. What you write down doesn't have to be perfect, polished, or permanent. Give yourself permission to capture very rough ideas. Use the space to just sketch or map out what seems true for you today, knowing that you will edit as you go. It's okay if you feel unsure or insecure about your answers. This model is intended to help you continually clarify who you are at each level. What's most important is that you slow down and recognize and capture your *current* thinking. Doing so can raise the right questions and help generate some appropriate next actions.

There's a hunger in me that always wants to be creating and orating, telling people something and giving them information and getting feedback. There are so many questions that I'm trying to ask, and I'm still so far from being done saying what I gotta say.

—CHANCE THE RAPPER

Purpose Map

PURPOSE

I feel I'm on the planet to _____.

(File away in your PURPOSE folder.)

VISION

The Vision level involves imagining what you'd like to have be true in the future. This could include what you want to have happen in high school, after high school, in college, and beyond. Here's the key question for this level: If you were wildly successful in the coming years, what do you imagine or see yourself doing?

Using the Vision map on the following page, take some time to capture your ideal scenario. Think big! Think wild success! Write notes, generate ideas, cut out and tape pictures, make lists, insert quotes, and capture any other piece of information that represents success for you. If you like working with digital tools (computer, tablet, phone), copy and paste images. Your goal is to fill up the map with your *ideal* future—from who you will be, to whom you'll be with, to what you'll be doing.

Success is about dedication. You may not be where you want to be or do what you want to do when you're on the journey. But you've got to be willing to have vision and foresight that leads you to an incredible end.   —USHER

Vision Map

VISION

Here's a vivid picture, drawing, and/or description of what my future will look and feel like.

(File away in your VISION folder.)

GOALS

Take a look at back at what you captured for your Purpose and Vision maps. What do they inspire you to do in your life this year? Are there some bigger items that you'd like to check off as having been completed? By when?

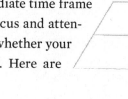

These are the types of items to place at the Goals level. Goals are larger aspirations with a somewhat more immediate time frame that help you to determine *where* to put your focus and attention. This level can also assist you in assessing whether your goals connect up to your Vision and Purpose. Here are some examples of goals:

- Graduate from high school.
- Start a band.
- Create an app.
- Graduate from college.
- Make the high school varsity team.
- Start a successful YouTube channel.

- Get my driver's license.
- Climb a mountain.
- Get the lead part in the play.
- Graduate in the top 10 percent of my class.

Using the Goals map on the following page, capture some items that are important to you right now and can be potentially completed and checked off as done. Write down the "What" and put a check in the appropriate "When" section.

Setting goals is the first step in turning the invisible into the visible.

—TONY ROBBINS

Goals Map

GOALS

I would like to (what)   by   (when)

	1 month	1 semester	1 year	1+ years

(File away in your GOALS folder.)

I don't focus on what I'm up against.
I focus on my goals and I try to ignore the rest.   —VENUS WILLIAMS

AREAS OF FOCUS

The Areas of Focus level enables you to track the major parts of life that *continually* need your attention that you are committed to *maintain*.

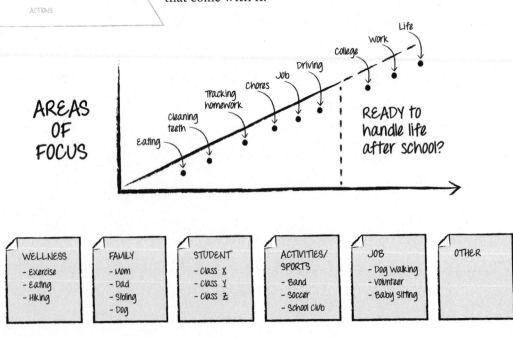

Because the areas of life that you're responsible for shift and grow over time, this level becomes very dynamic as you grow older. You'll go through many transitions, likely even within a single year. Areas of focus change as you move from a state of dependence on the adults in your life to a state of independence—to *freedom*. You gradually take on more of the responsibilities for which adults are currently responsible.

For example, an adult may now take care of your transportation, driving you around to where you need to go. Within a few years, you might take on that role yourself with all the obligations that come with it.

Creating, reviewing, and maintaining your Areas of Focus will help you achieve a sense of clarity, balance, and calm. They will also build your confidence in learning to handle life after high school and college. Identifying and managing your Areas of Focus will also help others build trust and confidence in you.

As you grow older, you might find that this level includes areas that do not change much over time:

- I am a son/daughter.
- I am a brother/sister.

You'll also discover areas that change at a faster pace:

- Middle school student expectations to high school student expectations
- From not driving to driving
- From not having a job to having a job
- From not paying attention to your health and well-being to taking control of them

Using the Areas of Focus map, capture what you see as the key Areas of Focus that are part of your life *today*. We've included some common ones as starting points.

Are there other areas *you* need to pay attention to and maintain? What responsibilities will transfer from parents or teachers to you in the near future?

Accountability breeds response-ability. —STEPHEN COVEY

Areas of Focus Map

AREAS OF FOCUS

Over time AREAS OF FOCUS transfer from adults in your life (parents, teachers, coaches) to you. Keeping an eye on your AREAS OF FOCUS will help you handle <u>any</u> transitions in your life.

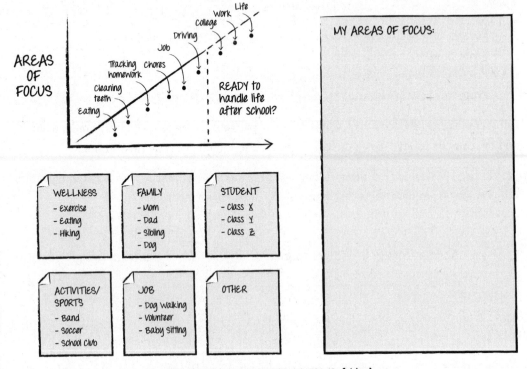

(File away in your AREAS OF FOCUS folder.)

PAUSE AND REVERSE DIRECTION

Up to this point you've captured the first draft of your Purpose, Vision, Goals, and Areas of Focus. These are the *higher* levels. These levels will help *inform* the projects and actions you choose on a day-to-day and week-to-week basis.

Before we discuss the last two levels, let's briefly reverse direction. Take a couple of moments to look back at the content you captured for each level. Doing so may trigger some clarity that will inspire you to update each level with any new ideas.

- As you look at your Areas of Focus, do they trigger any new goals you might want to add to your Goals map?
- As you look at your Areas of Focus and Goals, do they trigger any new elements you want to add to your Vision map?
- As you look at your Areas of Focus, Goals, and Vision maps, are there any edits or adjustments you'd like to make to your Purpose map?

Did you add or edit anything? Or did you look at your result and decide, "Looks good for now"?

On the way down, the writer part of your brain did the work. Did your brain work differently in any way going *up* the Levels of Focus? As you went back up the levels, the editor part of your brain was engaged.

How does this happen?

The magic occurs when you get the ideas out of your brain into an external system (the Levels of Focus maps), so you are able to reflect on and review them. That system holds the right cues, which you will notice at the right time, about the right things, that are important to you.

Let's complete the journey down the levels by taking a look at projects and actions.

> Great things are not done by impulse, but by
> a series of small things brought together. —VINCENT VAN GOGH

Projects and Actions

In the previous section on the Five Steps, breaking down actionable stuff into projects and actions takes place during the clarify step. Projects get organized on your projects list, and actions go on your calendar or next action list. These are the bottom two levels on the Levels of Focus. During the Five Steps, you'll be constantly adding material to them.

The pyramid is labeled, from top to bottom: PURPOSE, VISION, GOALS, AREAS OF FOCUS, PROJECTS, ACTIONS.

Some projects may come to you with a well-defined structure (e.g., complete book report for English by next Tuesday). Others may require *you* to define what "done" looks like (e.g., research paper submitted, land a summer job, community volunteer project completed, song recorded). The latter are examples of "make it up, make it happen" type of projects. Over time these may constitute the majority of what's on your projects list.

Actions define what you need to *do* and refers to all the physical, visible actions you can take. This level is often referred to as the runway level. It's where the rubber meets the road. (For example, do Chapter Two math exercises, wash the dog, pick up my room, drop off signed form with teacher, write first draft of book report, practice piano.)

Your project, calendar, and next action lists, which you created in the Five Step section of the book, serve as your maps for these bottom two Levels of Focus.

> The way to get started is to quit talking and begin doing.
> —WALT DISNEY

Projects and Actions Map

PROJECTS AND NEXT ACTIONS

Your AREAS OF FOCUS, and higher horizons, hold your focus and direction.

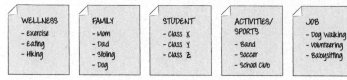

WELLNESS
- Exercise
- Eating
- Hiking

FAMILY
- Mom
- Dad
- Sibling
- Dog

STUDENT
- Class X
- Class Y
- Class Z

ACTIVITIES/ SPORTS
- Band
- Soccer
- School Club

JOB
- Dog Walking
- Volunteering
- Babysitting

OTHER

Your Projects List holds your outcomes that will take more than one next action.

"Projects help us define the finish line, what "DONE" looks like."

PROJECTS
- ☐ Explore
- ☐ Design
- ☐ Create
- ☐ Build
- ☐ Learn

"Actions help us define what "DOING" looks like."

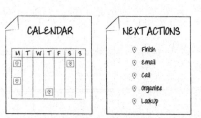

CALENDAR

M	T	W	T	F	S	S

NEXT ACTIONS
- ⊙ Finish
- ⊙ Email
- ⊙ Call
- ⊙ Organize
- ⊙ Lookup

(File away in PROJECTS & ACTIONS in your planner, agenda, or folders.)

Do or do not. There is no try.   —YODA

LEVELS OF FOCUS WRAP-UP

After filling out these six Levels of Focus for the first time, you'll have a working first draft that will assist you in gaining a deeper perspective by connecting your actions to the things you have determined are important to you.

If you haven't captured anything yet or feel that some of your levels are incomplete, don't worry. You now know that these levels exist, and you've had the initial experience traveling up and down the six levels. The level maps will be waiting for you to capture or edit your thoughts and ideas when *you* are ready.

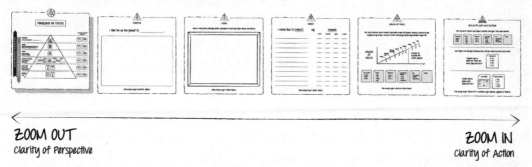

ZOOM OUT
Clarity of Perspective

ZOOM IN
Clarity of Action

Here are some tips for using your Levels of Focus:

- If you're feeling a bit stuck in life or are facing a problem or tough decision and need more clarity on which direction to go, try *moving up* the Levels of Focus to gain *clarity*.
- If you're feeling that you know where you want to go but are having trouble getting your idea into motion or don't see the results that you were hoping for, try *moving down* the Levels of Focus to help generate and translate the idea into *actions*.
- Consider adding your Levels of Focus maps into your weekly review. These maps can serve as triggers and ensure you continue to ask yourself questions at different levels.

Every time you review, reflect upon, and update your Levels of Focus, you connect the dots between your Purpose–Vision–Goals–Areas of Focus to your Projects–Actions. This creates the conditions for you to bring the fullest, most creative, most awesome version of you to the world.

SUMMARY

LEVELS OF FOCUS

ADDITIONAL SUPPORT MATERIALS

If you need more clarity, go up the Horizons of Focus.

If you need more action, move down the Horizons of Focus.

PURPOSE
I feel I'm on the planet to _____ .

NOTES MY PURPOSE

CHECKLIST   REFERENCE (GENERAL)

VISION
Pictures, drawings and/or notes of my ideal scene for myself in the future.

NOTES OR PICTURES VISION

CHECKLIST   REFERENCE (GENERAL)

GOALS
I want to achieve (what) by (when).

LIST GOALS

CHECKLIST   REFERENCE (GENERAL)

AREAS OF FOCUS
My main areas of responsibilities.

FAMILY   SON/DAUGHTER   STUDENT   LIST AREAS OF FOCUS   WELLNESS   SPIRITUALITY   SPORTS   ACTIVITIES

CHECKLIST   REFERENCE (GENERAL)

PROJECTS
My short term desired outcomes.

PROJECTS   SOMEDAY/MAYBE LIST

CHECKLIST   REFERENCE (GENERAL)

ACTION
Doing.

CALENDAR   NEXT ACTIONS

CHECKLIST   REFERENCE (GENERAL)

The Levels of Focus offers a model that can help you achieve perspective. It consists of six levels. Each provides a different perspective on your life, and moving between them can help gain clarity or increase action.

KEY TERMS

- Levels of Focus
- Purpose
- Vision
- Goals
- Areas of Focus

QUESTIONS FOR THOUGHT OR DISCUSSION

- At which level do you spend most of your time thinking? At which level do you spend the least amount of time thinking?
- Which level is the hardest for you to clarify at this point in your life?
- Is there something in your life that could use more clarity or more action for which you could apply the Levels of Focus model?
- Which level do you think is the most difficult for others your age? Why?

PROJECT PLANNING: THE PLANNING MAP

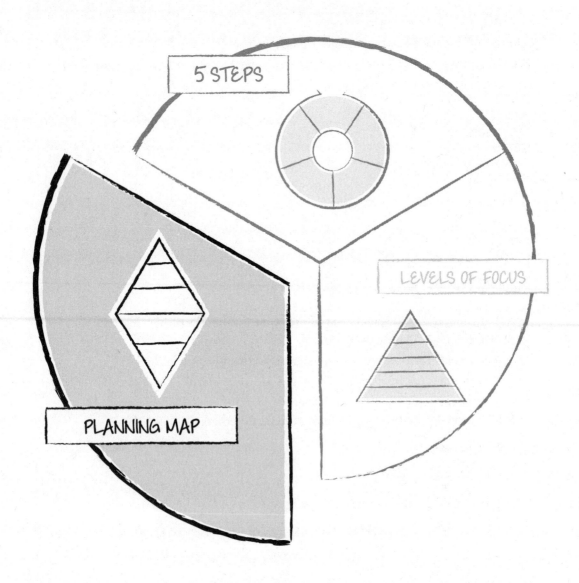

5 STEPS

LEVELS OF FOCUS

PLANNING MAP

The Planning Map

In the first part of the book you learned the Five Steps and how they can help you gain control. Using the Five Steps can also get you back to ready when necessary.

In the second part you worked on your Levels of Focus and explored how they might help you gain perspective. You learned how to use the levels by zooming out and zooming in.

In the third part, we'll introduce you to the final tool in the GTD system, the Planning Map.

The Planning Map is a simple yet powerful thinking tool. It can help you work your way through any situation—like writing a paper, solving a problem, writing a college essay, working with your classmates on a project, or preparing for a class presentation, all with less effort and better results. Let's explore what makes this tool so powerful.

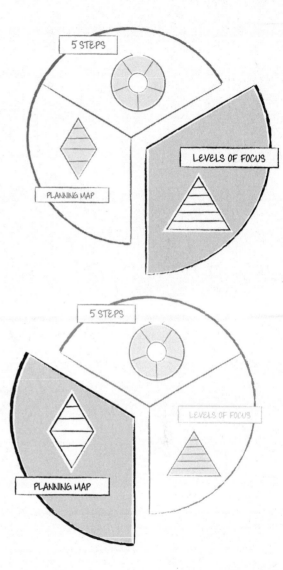

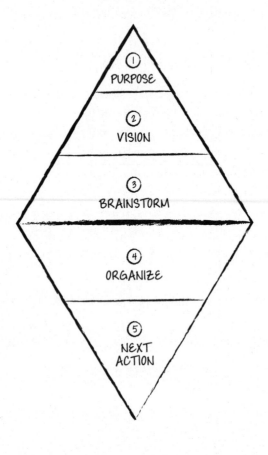

PLANNING MAP

① PURPOSE

② VISION

③ BRAINSTORM

④ ORGANIZE

⑤ NEXT ACTION

Natural Planning

Our brain is a truly spectacular tool. Every human-made creation began with an idea from the brain. The Planning Map was designed to work in much the same way your brain naturally functions, planning in a process so quick and natural that you may not even notice it. The Planning Map consists of five steps, which your mind automatically goes through when you seek to accomplish almost any task or desired outcome:

1. Define purpose, principles, and standards
2. Outcome visioning
3. Brainstorming
4. Organizing
5. Identifying next actions

Let's look at an example that shows how these steps occur naturally.

It is Friday night, and you want to go to the movies with your friends. Notice that there is already an established desired outcome: "go to the movies with friends." As you learned during the Five Steps section, your brain does well with clearly defined outcomes, as it creates a picture of what you want to have be true. This sets the stage for your brain to kick into planning mode and requests key information like, "Why go to the movies? What first caused you to think about going to the movies?"

There could be any number of answers to these questions, such as:

- You might want to hang out with friends.
- You may be excited to watch the next installment of a movie series.
- You might want to sit close to that someone special you've admired in math class.

The "why" defines your purpose, and it ignites the internal planning process. In this example, let's say you decide your purpose is to hang out with friends.

Your brain then moves on to the next question: Are there any standards to follow? Standards create the boundaries for planning, and your brain will limit your thinking to these particular standards and boundaries. Your parents might have told you, "You can go to the movies so long as you are back by ten p.m." That is a standard that frames your thinking and planning.

Purpose and standards define the boundaries for getting from where you are to your outcome.

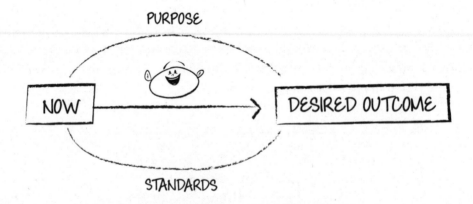

Once you've identified your desired outcome, purpose, and standards, your brain asks, "What is your vision of wild success? How do you see the story playing out?"

Perhaps your answers are something like this:

- Laughing and having fun with your friends
- Getting great seats for the movie
- Enjoying some snacks
- Looking good

Your vision for the night is now established.

As your purpose, standards, and vision become set, your brain generates information to help you move toward your desired outcome of going to the movies. It starts to download information, in no specific order. This random download is natural, and its randomness is normal. This is called brainstorming. Some examples:

- What time is the movie?
- What am I going to wear?
- How much money should I bring?
- Who else is going?
- What time will we meet?
- Is my favorite red shirt clean?

These questions occur as part of the creative process that takes place after you've committed to an outcome.

Once you've generated enough ideas and details, your brain instinctively starts to organize them:

- First, I need to find out which movies are playing.
- Next, I need to confirm who can go.
- I need to get a ride to and from the movie theater.
- I need to call my friend to see if I can borrow his jacket.

Finally, if you are committed to going to the movies, you'll shift focus on the next action to take to make this happen.

- I need to send a group chat to friends with movie and time options.

The following five phases of planning occur naturally for everything that you accomplish during the day:

1. You have the urge to make something happen.
2. You imagine the outcome.
3. You generate ideas that might be relevant.
4. You sort those into some structure.
5. You define a physical, visible action that will begin to make it a reality.

The amazing thing is that you generally do this without giving it much thought, so why not apply this process elsewhere? You can capture this power and replicate it in any situation by using the Planning Map.

The Planning Map

The Planning Map is a tool that can help harness the power of this natural thinking process.

It can greatly support you in getting your bigger plans (e.g., book reports, community projects, scouting efforts, science projects, etc.) done in less time with better results. The Planning Map can bring clarity to any project, situation, or intention, and the more you use it, the better you will get with it. And the better you get, the more you will *want* to use it.

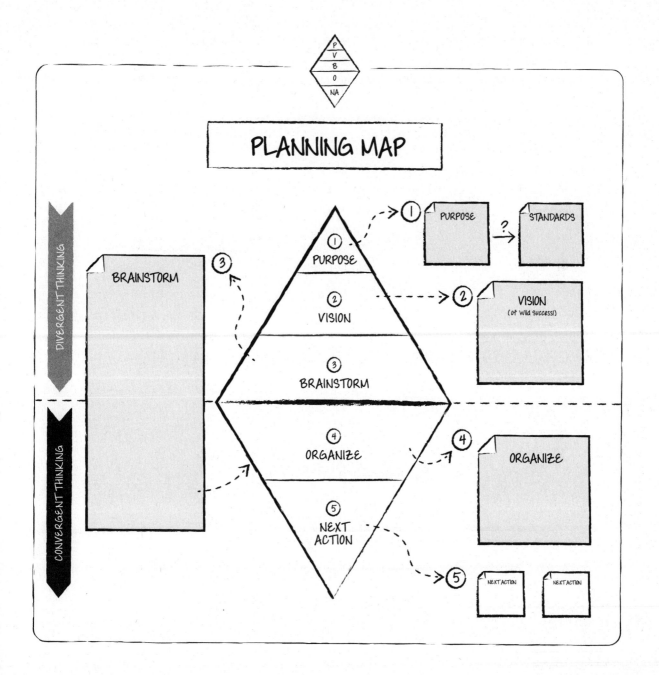

PLANNING MAP

To help introduce the components of the Planning Map, let's imagine a friend named Megan, who has a research paper to finish. It will take her more than one next action to complete, so she comes up with a project name and adds it to her projects list.

Project: Hand in a solid research paper on giant squids

With the outcome defined, let's look at what it might be like for her to think through the project using the Planning Map.

1. PURPOSE/GUIDING PRINCIPLES

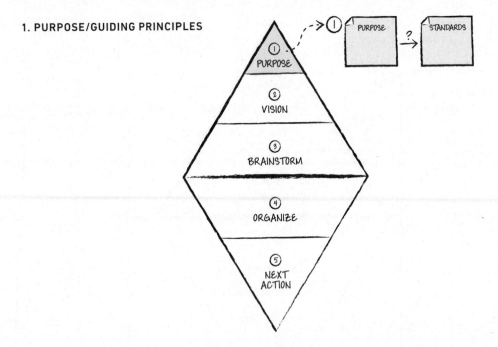

Purpose describes the point of the action: "Why I am doing this?"

Standards defines the boundaries: "What are the rules?"

Megan begins by considering her purpose. Using the map, she thinks for a while and then writes:

To present a really good paper about something that interests me—giant squids. This book report is also a big chunk of my grade—50 percent. I want to put my best effort into it so I can get a good grade in this class.

Moving to the next part of the map, she asks herself, "Are there any standards to keep in mind?"

She captures the following standards:

> The teacher stated that it must be original work—no copying from the Internet or anyplace else. She also said it had to be five hundred words, typed and double-spaced.

With her purpose and standards clarified, Megan moves to the vision section of the Planning Map.

2. VISION/DESIRED OUTCOME

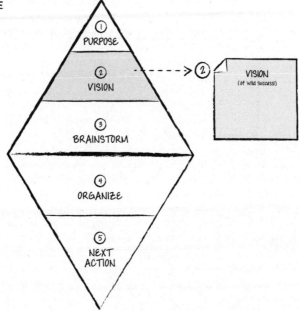

Vision describes the goal in detail. What will wild success look and feel like? For Megan, this means:

> The research paper is so interesting that the teacher will pull me aside and say, "Well done! This was fascinating!" I'm also going to apply what I learned from my last paper to this project. Specifically, I'm not going to submit a first draft. I'm going to proofread my initial draft and also have someone else proof it. Then I'll make updates and hand in my second or third draft.

3. BRAINSTORM

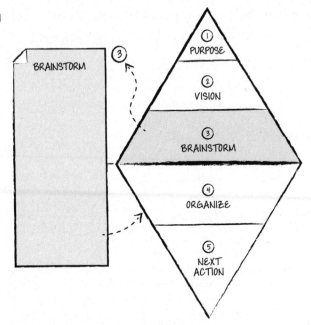

Brainstorming begins to generate and lay out all the pieces. What are all the thoughts that occur about making this happen?

With her vision of wild success defined, Megan shifts her focus to the left side of the map and writes down all the ideas that come to her that could potentially help make her vision come true.

- Get several books on squids from the library.
- Search YouTube for giant squid videos.
- Search Google for pictures and images.
- Get index cards for the project.
- Schedule time in my calendar to work on the paper.
- Interview a squid expert?
- Ask John if he will proofread my drafts.

Megan pauses and is pleased by the progress she's made in such a short amount of time. With some solid brainstorming completed, she is ready to move to the next part of the map.

4. ORGANIZE

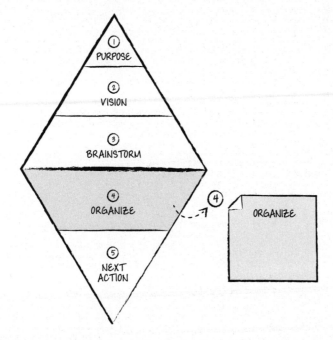

Organizing describes the components, categories, or order of events needed to achieve the goal. For some school projects, a teacher may give you templates to help you organize your thoughts (e.g., book report templates, science lab report templates).

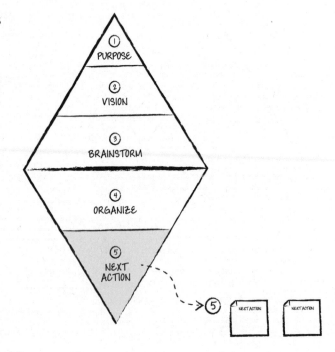

Looking at the items on her brainstorm list, Megan sees a few natural groupings and starts sorting the items into categories.

- Research: Get several books on squids from library, search YouTube for giant squid videos, find pictures, and interview a squid expert.
- Writing: Get index cards for project and schedule time in my calendar to work on the paper.
- Proofreading: Ask John if he will proofread my drafts.

She quickly checks this plan against her purpose, principles, standards, and vision. Everything looks good, and she feels comfortably on track.

5. NEXT ACTIONS

Now, Megan is ready to move and generates the next action(s) needed for the project.

Looking over the plan she organized, she quickly identifies one:

Search YouTube for giant squid videos.

She adds this to her next action list to be completed later, because she's due at tennis practice. On her way there, she notices that she is much calmer than she was during her last practice. She feels she's made some good progress, even though she has more work to do before she's done.

One more thought occurs to her: She has a group history project that is currently stalled, and she wants a good grade on that, too. Using her phone, she captures a note for her digital inbox.

Try the Planning Map with group history project.

Presto! It's now in her system for follow-up.

She arrives at tennis practice with a clear head and one thing on her mind: tennis. She is *ready*.

Planning Map in Action

The best way to learn about the Planning Map is to play with and practice it. Here are some examples of how you might put the Planning Map into action:

- Planning adventures for the summer break with your family
- Sketching out a practice plan for your favorite sport or activity
- Writing a college application essay
- Creating or updating your Areas of Focus
- Creating or updating your Goals

You can also use the map along with different capture and organizing tools. Examples:

- Create a mind map.
- Use Post-it notes on a wall.
- Use a large whiteboard.
- Use a large corkboard.

What ideas does *your* spectacular brain have for our world? Use this model and the clear space you've created to bring them to life!

This world is but a canvas to our imagination.

—HENRY DAVID THOREAU

SUMMARY

The Planning Map is a tool that can help you gain control of and perspective on almost anything. It is mainly used for projects but can also be applied to higher levels on the Levels of Focus. The Planning Map mimics the natural way your brain plans for things. It has five distinct stages, and each stage has a process associated with it.

KEY TERMS

- Planning Map
- Brainstorm

QUESTIONS FOR THOUGHT OR DISCUSSION

- What in your life right now could benefit from the use of the Planning Map?
- Looking back, what other projects might have benefitted from using the map?

CONCLUSION

Ready to Win Where You Are Going

So there you have it. Learn to pay attention to what has your attention. Listen to the signals from your brain. Watch out for pitfalls.

Gain control over stuff by engaging in the Five Steps.

 Use the Levels of Focus to help you gain perspective.

 Project plan using the Planning Map.

 Achieve control and perspective.

Find the ready state.

Now that you are **ready**, what will you do with this new-found **control** and **perspective**?

What do you want to have be *true* that isn't?

What do you *want to do* more than anything else?

What *impact* do you want to make on the world?

Have an answer?

Good.

Go . . . make it happen . . .
you are indeed **READY**.

We believe in you.

The world is but a canvas to our imagination.

—HENRY DAVID THOREAU

Part 3
The Lab

Additional Examples
and Things to Try

THE LAB

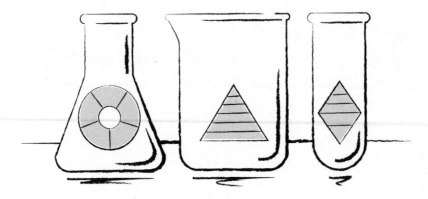

Welcome to THE LAB!

You can think of this section of the book as a place to find life hacks—ideas that you can try, modify, and integrate into your own trusted system. Are you stressed? Do you find you get inspired when you go for a walk? We've got ideas for you to test on both. You can determine how helpful this collection of situation-specific experiments is for you, taking what works and skipping what doesn't. Each of the labs has proven to be beneficial to someone somewhere.

As a first step, we recommend you do a quick scan of the labs and see if any of them immediately resonate with you. Start small, and when you find an item you'd like to test, try it out. Come back and visit the labs occasionally. Your circumstances and experience levels change over time. You may find that different labs can have an impact on you at different stages of your life or during times of transition.

Have fun experimenting!

FIVE STEPS

Try a Walking Mind Sweep

QUESTION:

Do you find you think better when you are moving?

RELATED TO:

Step 1: Capture

THE JOB IT DOES:

It removes distractions and clears your mind in a different way.
It works well for people who think better when they are moving.

WHAT TO DO:

Go for a walk outside (ten to fifteen minutes can be enough). Bring a capture tool with you. Try to have a capturing tool that won't add any distraction (e.g., alerts on your phone). Walk and relax and allow your mind to wander. If you land on something that needs your attention, write it down. Continue throughout your walk.

EXPERIMENT:

Try a week without doing a walking mind sweep.

Try a week where you do a short walking mind sweep each day.

NOTICE:

How do you feel without your walk?

How did you feel with your walk?

How many items did you capture?

Did you notice anything similar or different about your walks each day?

Try Capturing into a *Big* Bucket

QUESTION:

Do you have an area that is out of control or really needs some work? A closet? Car? Sports bag? Drawer? Locker?

RELATED TO:

Step 1: Capture

Step 2: Clarify

THE JOB IT DOES:

Clears an area that is troublesome or chaotic with very minimal effort.

WHAT TO DO:

Get a large, temporary bucket like a laundry basket or plastic tub. Instead of "cleaning" the space by going through one thing at a time, just remove everything that doesn't belong in that space and throw it in the large bucket. Don't make any decisions about the stuff or organize it elsewhere. Just clear the space of all stuff and then put that bucket somewhere. Take whatever stuff you see in the bucket through the clarify step (Transforming Tool) to process later.

EXPERIMENT:

Try clearing a small space that you've been meaning to get to (e.g., drawer).
Try clearing a larger space (e.g., closet, garage, basement).

NOTICE:

How do you feel about the space after clearing it?
How much time did it take?
Was stuff in the space easier to deal with after being taken out and put in a bucket?

Try Capturing Your Stress

QUESTION:

Do you feel stressed or overloaded?

RELATED TO:

Step 1: Capture
Step 2: Clarify

THE JOB IT DOES:

Writing down the things that are causing you stress captures them on paper. Once you have them visible on paper, your brain can see them. Once your brain sees them, it can start the process of determining what actions are needed to resolve them.

WHAT TO DO:

Grab a pen and paper and start writing, or sit with a friend and just tell them everything that is on your mind and is triggering stress. Have them capture everything you are saying without saying anything other than asking clarifying questions. Don't try to resolve anything yet. Just get it all out of your head. Next, look at the list you generated. Take whatever stuff you see on that list through the clarify step (Transforming Tool) to process later.

EXPERIMENT:

Try this type of mind sweep alone.
Try it with a partner.

NOTICE:

How do you feel dumping everything during the mind sweep?
How do you feel after clarifying?

Try Capturing Your Worry

QUESTION:

Are you worried?

RELATED TO:

Step 1: Capture
Step 2: Clarify

THE JOB IT DOES:

It helps offload the stuff on your mind using a mind sweep.

Grab a pen and paper and start writing, or sit with a friend and just tell them everything that is on your mind and is triggering stress. Have them capture everything you are saying without saying anything other than asking clarifying questions. Don't try to resolve anything yet. Just get it all out of your head. Next, look at the list you generated. Take whatever stuff you see on that list through the clarify step (Transforming Tool) to process later.

EXPERIMENT:

Try this type of mind sweep alone.
Try it with a partner.

NOTICE:

How do you feel dumping everything during the mind sweep?
How do you feel after clarifying?

Try a Mind Sweep before Bed

QUESTION:

Are you having a hard time falling asleep?

RELATED TO:

Step 1: Capture

THE JOB IT DOES:

Writing down the things that are on your mind before you go to bed may help you let go of them. Once you have them visible on paper, your brain can see them. Once your brain sees them, it can relax.

WHAT TO DO:

Grab a pen and paper and write down the things on your mind.
Don't try to resolve anything yet. Just get it all out of your head.
In the morning, take whatever stuff you see on that list through the clarify step (Trans-
forming Tool).

EXPERIMENT:

Try this type of mind sweep for several days.
Try it with a partner.

NOTICE:

How does it feel to capture the things that have your attention?
How do you feel after doing it for several days?

Try Placing a Capture Tool by Your Bed

QUESTION:

Do you have thoughts or ideas that are waking you up during the night?

RELATED TO:

Step 1: Capture

THE JOB IT DOES:

Writing down things that are waking you up may help you let go of them and get back
to sleep. The more you do it, the more your brain will trust that it will see it in the
morning. Once you have them visible on paper, your brain can see them.

WHAT TO DO:

Place a pen and paper next to your bed.
If you are woken up by a thought, write it down.
Try to go back to sleep.
In the morning, take whatever stuff you wrote down and put it in your "in" box.
Bring these items through the clarify step (Transforming Tool).

EXPERIMENT:

Place a pen and paper by your bed. Write down the things that are waking you up.

NOTICE:

What happened when you wrote down things and then went back to sleep?
How do you feel after doing it for several days?

Try Creating a Reading Plan

QUESTION:

Do you have a large reading project to complete?

RELATED TO:

Planning Map
Step 4: Organize

THE JOB IT DOES:

It helps you organize a large reading assignment (novel, textbook, etc.) into an actionable plan.

WHAT TO DO:

Take out your calendar and the book that you want to read.

Pick a target date on your calendar for finishing the book.

Count the number of days until that target date.

Divide the number of pages in your book by the number of days until the target date.

Fill in your calendar with the page number you should be on each day to follow that plan.

> For example: 200-page book/10 days to read = 20 pages per day. Day 1: p. 20, Day 2: p. 40, Day 3: p. 60, etc.

This plan on your calendar becomes a map to let you know how much to read each day and helps you feel comfortable reading and *not* reading.

EXPERIMENT:

Try breaking up a large reading project using this method.

NOTICE:

How do you feel about your plan?

Did your plan make you feel more comfortable when you were *not* reading?

How do you feel each day trying to follow the plan vs. trying to just "read the book"?

Did you need to break your day goal into more than one reading session?

Try a Backpack Unpack/Repack

QUESTION:

Do you know what's in your backpack?

RELATED TO:

Step 1: Capture

Step 2: Clarify

THE JOB IT DOES:

It helps you remove clutter from your backpack, helps you identify actionable stuff (e.g., a form that needs signing by a parent), and sets you up for success between home and school.

WHAT TO DO:

Grab the backpack or bag that you bring to school.
Start by dumping everything out of it.
Determine what is REDS. The rest is stuff.
Bring the stuff through the clarify step (Transforming Tool).
Organize accordingly into actionable and nonactionable piles.
Capture or do any next actions from your actionable pile.

EXPERIMENT:

Try a backpack repack on a Sunday before the start of the school week.
Try a backpack unpack/repack on Friday when you get home from school.

NOTICE:

Did you find any actionable stuff in your backpack?
Did you find any trash?
How did you feel when you were done?
Did it have any impact on you during the week?

Try the Post-it Note Hack for Your Planner

QUESTION:

Do you have a planner that was given to you or required of you by your school? Does it have the lists/maps you need? If not, hack it!

RELATED TO:

Step 1: Capture
Step 3: Organize
Step 4: Reflect

THE JOB IT DOES:

Update your planner so it contains all your key lists—Next Actions, Projects, Someday/Maybe.

WHAT TO DO:

Most planners have a calendar of some sort.
Insert a Post-it note to capture ideas.
Insert a Post-it note for your next action list.
Insert a Post-it note for your projects list.
Insert a Post-it note for your someday/maybe list.
Any planner in any form can be hacked into a GTD planner.

EXPERIMENT:

Update your planner with Post-it notes for your key lists.

NOTICE:

What's working? What isn't?
How does it feel to have one place for all your lists?
Does having all your lists in one place help you with your weekly review?

Try Using the Five Steps for Your Musical Ideas

QUESTION:

Do you have musical ideas in your head? Do you have many unfinished musical projects?

RELATED TO:

Step 1: Capture
Step 2: Clarify
Step 3: Organize
Step 5: Engage

THE JOB IT DOES:

It helps you take the ideas from your head and puts them into your trusted external system.

WHAT TO DO:

Capture your musical ideas using a recording app on your phone or a voice recorder.
Create a special musical idea inbox (e.g., a folder on your computer to store MP3 files).
Set up a time to input your ideas using the clarify step.
Organize your musical projects into unique project folders (e.g., Song 1, Song 2).
Create a projects list for your song ideas.
Determine the next action needed to move a song forward (e.g., record bridge for song 2).

EXPERIMENT:

Try setting up a capture/clarify/organize system for your musical ideas.

NOTICE:

Is musical stuff any different than other types of stuff?

How does it feel to have a capture system for your musical ideas?

How might you use the Planning Map for your musical ideas?

Try Capture/Clarify/Organize with a Friend

QUESTION:

Do you enjoy working with others? Do you have a friend or mentor who feels the same?

RELATED TO:

Step 1: Capture

Step 2: Clarify

Step 3: Organize

THE JOB IT DOES:

It helps you practice the *fundamental thinking process*, provides accountability, and offers you a new way of looking at your process.

WHAT TO DO:

Find a friend, mentor, or family member who would be willing to partner with you.

Spend five minutes capturing what has your attention by writing it down and placing it into your bucket.

For every item you captured, have your partner walk you through the clarify step (Transforming Tool).

Have your partner ensure that you are making clear decisions that transform your stuff and lead to specific next actions.

Continue until you finish your list.

Now switch roles and offer the same service to your partner!

EXPERIMENT:

Try to capture/clarify/organize with a partner.

Try to capture/clarify/organize alone.

Try it with a partner.

NOTICE:

How were the experiences different?

How did it feel when your partner guided you through the Transformation Tool?

How did it feel when you guided your partner through the Transformation Tool?

Try Doing a Weekly Review with a Partner

QUESTION:

Do you enjoy working with others? Do you have a friend or mentor who feels the same?

RELATED TO:

Step 4: Reflect

THE JOB IT DOES:

It helps you practice the weekly review.

WHAT TO DO:

Find a friend or family member who would be willing to partner with you.

Go through the steps of the weekly review together.

Try a weekly review alone.
Try it with a partner.

NOTICE:

How were the experiences different?
Which did you prefer?
What questions emerged from your weekly review?

Try Timed "Doing" Sprints

QUESTION:

Do you sometimes struggle with procrastination?

RELATED TO:

Step 5: Engage

THE JOB IT DOES:

It helps you focus on "doing" for short periods of time rather than focusing on completion.

WHAT TO DO:

Set a countdown timer for five, ten, or fifteen minutes.
Choose an action (e.g., reading).
Start your timer.
Put your full effort and focus into your chosen action until the timer rings.

When that sprint is complete, take a short break (e.g., five minutes).
Conduct a second timed sprint.
Continue sprints until you have run out of time or energy.

EXPERIMENT:

Try doing your homework from start to finish with no breaks.
Try doing your homework in sprints with breaks included.

NOTICE:

How do you feel working from start to finish?
How did you feel doing your work with sprints and breaks?
Which did you prefer?

Try Generating Momentum by Cleaning up a Small Area

QUESTION:

Do you feel stalled and don't know where to begin?

RELATED TO:

Step 5: Engage

THE JOB IT DOES:

It creates a win when your energy and focus levels are low.

WHAT TO DO:

Find a small area or thing that needs cleaning or organizing (e.g., folding laundry).
Organize the area (capture/clarify/organize).

Continue until the area is organized.

Tip: Make it fun. Play music or watch TV.

EXPERIMENT:

Clean or organize a small area.

NOTICE:

How long did it take you to clean or organize the area?

How did you feel before?

How did you feel after?

Try Time Blocking "Playing Cards"

QUESTION:

Is the thought of starting on your homework repelling you?

RELATED TO:

Step 5: Engage

THE JOB IT DOES:

It helps you allocate time and focus attention on specific things for shorter periods of time.

WHAT TO DO:

Grab some index cards.

Write "10" on each card, which will represent ten-minute blocks.

Using Post-it notes, write down the assignments or action you need to finish.

Next, grab the number of "10" cards that represents the amount of time you have. (If you have sixty minutes, grab six cards.)

Now "deal" the cards onto the Post-its, deciding how many ten-minute blocks to dedicate to each action. For example, three cards on "Study for Science Test," one card on "Practice Flash Cards," one for "Break," etc.

Now set a timer and spend your set amount of time on each.

EXPERIMENT:

Try doing your homework from start to finish with no breaks.
Try doing your homework using playing cards.

NOTICE:

How do you feel working from start to finish?
How did you feel working in ten-minute blocks?
Which did you prefer?

Try Creating an Action Card

QUESTION:

You have thirty minutes to make progress on something. What do you do?

RELATED TO:

Step 5: Engage

THE JOB IT DOES:

It helps you focus during short windows of time.

WHAT TO DO:

Grab an index card.

Do a review of your calendar and next action lists.

Pick two to three items you can complete in a short period of time (e.g., email, sign-ups, etc.).

Write those things on the card as check boxes.

EXPERIMENT:

Try engaging in a short period of time without a quick action list.

Try engaging in a short period of time with a quick action list.

NOTICE:

Which did you prefer?

Was it easier or harder to focus without a quick action list?

Try a Walking Brainstorm

QUESTION:

How do I capture a bunch of ideas about my project (e.g., write a paper about what I did this summer)?

RELATED TO:

Step 3: Brainstorm

Planning Map

THE JOB IT DOES:

It captures ideas triggered by the Purpose and Vision for your project.

WHAT TO DO:

Get a capture tool (e.g., index cards). Try to have a capture tool that won't add any additional distraction (e.g., alerts on your phone).

Go for a walk outside. (Ten to fifteen minutes can be enough.)

Focus on your topic.

Walk and relax and allow your mind to wander. As it lands on an idea, write it down. Continue capturing your ideas throughout your walk.

You are now ready to start step 4: Organize.

EXPERIMENT:

Try working on a project without doing a Walking Brainstorm.

Try working on a project with a Walking Brainstorm.

NOTICE:

How many minutes was your walk?

How many ideas did you generate?

Did the change of environment help with your creativity?

Try Capturing/Clarifying/Organizing Your Room (Instead of Picking It Up)

QUESTION:

Have you ever wished you could organize your room with the least amount of effort?

RELATED TO:

Step 1: Capture

Step 2: Clarify

Step 3: Organize

THE JOB IT DOES:

It gets your room clean with the least amount of effort!

WHAT TO DO:

Grab a big bucket and do a stuff hunt in your room.
Collect everything that isn't REDS.
Take one item out of your bucket at a time.
Ask yourself, "What is it?"
And, based on your answer, put it where it goes!

EXPERIMENT:

Try cleaning your room randomly.
Try cleaning your room using capture/clarify/organize steps.

NOTICE:

Which did you prefer?

Did you notice that stuff comes in different types of shapes, sizes, and forms?
Did the act of organizing your room trigger any mental stuff (e.g., I need a new picture
  for this frame)? Did you capture it?

CHECKLISTS

> Checklists . . . provide protection against such failures.
> They remind us of the minimum necessary steps
> and make them explicit. —ATUL GAWANDE, *THE CHECKLIST MANIFESTO*

Class Checklist

THE JOB IT DOES:

It helps you stay optimally engaged with your classes.

WHAT TO DO:

Draft a checklist of items specific to each class you need to review (e.g., Homework done? Next test? Extra credit available? Did I participate in class today? Bigger projects on track? Do I need to schedule time with the teacher for help?).
Review the list daily or as you enter your class.

EXPERIMENT:

For a week, go to class without a checklist.
For a few weeks, go to class with a checklist.

NOTICE:

How do you feel?
Did you notice any extra credit opportunities?
Did you participate more in class?
Did you have a conversation with your teacher outside of normal classroom activities?

Did you feel a "win!"?
Is there anything to add to your checklist?

Chore Checklist

THE JOB IT DOES:

It helps you get chores done with less time and less effort.

WHAT TO DO:

Draft a checklist of chores you need to do in your favorite list tool.

EXPERIMENT:

Do chores without a checklist.
Do chores with a checklist.

NOTICE:

How do you feel?
How much time did it take?
Did you feel a "win!"?
Did you forget anything? If yes, add it to the checklist.

Before-School Checklist

THE JOB IT DOES:

It helps you get out the door with less time and effort.
It reduces "Crap! I forgot [fill in the blank]." moments.

WHAT TO DO:

Draft a checklist of items you want to review before you leave for school.

EXPERIMENT:

Leave home without a Before-School checklist for a week.
Leave home with a Before-School checklist for a week.

NOTICE:

How do you feel with a checklist?
How did you feel without a checklist?
Did you feel a "win!"?
Did you forget anything?
If yes, what happened as a result?
If yes, add it to the checklist.

After-School Checklist

THE JOB IT DOES:

It helps you optimize your time, energy, and focus from the moment you depart school.

WHAT TO DO:

Draft a checklist of items you want to review after you leave school to help you stay appropriately focused and engaged. It might include time to relax, time to do homework, time to eat, time for activities, time to socialize, and time for family.

Leave school without an After-School checklist for a week.

Leave school with an After-School checklist for a week.

NOTICE:

How do you feel about your after-school time with a checklist?

How did you feel without a checklist?

Did you feel a "win!"?

Did you notice anything about your after-school time?

Sports Checklist

THE JOB IT DOES:

It reduces "Crap! I forgot my [fill in the blank]." moments.

It helps you leave home with all the gear you need to be successful in your sport.

WHAT TO DO:

Draft a checklist of items you need for your sport. Remember to include items that need signatures (e.g., permission slips).

EXPERIMENT:

Leave home without a Sports checklist for a week.

Leave home with a Sports checklist for a week.

NOTICE:

How do you feel about your readiness for your sport with a checklist?

How did you feel without a checklist?

Did you feel a "win!"?
Did you notice anything else?

Sports Skill Practice Checklist

THE JOB IT DOES:

It keeps your practice sessions focused and on track so you can optimize your skill development.

WHAT TO DO:

Draft a checklist of the important activities you need to practice to increase your skill for your sport.

EXPERIMENT:

Practice without a Sports Skill Practice checklist for a week.
Practice with a Sports Skill Practice checklist for a week.

NOTICE:

How do you feel about your skill development for your sport with a checklist?
How did you feel without a checklist?
Did you feel a "win!"?
Did you notice anything else?
Did any questions emerge?

Sports Pregame Checklist

THE JOB IT DOES:

It increases the ready state for your chosen sport.

WHAT TO DO:

Draft a checklist of the important reminders and activities you need to review or do to help get you optimally ready for competition.

EXPERIMENT:

Practice without a Sports Pregame checklist for a week.
Practice with a Sports Pregame checklist for a week.

NOTICE:

How do you feel about your competition readiness with a checklist?
How did you feel without a checklist?
Did you feel a "win!"?
Did you notice anything else?
Did any questions emerge?

Sports Postgame Checklist

THE JOB IT DOES:

It increases your capacity for reflection, noticing, and learning for your chosen sport.

WHAT TO DO:

Draft a checklist of the important reminders, questions, and activities you want to review after you complete a competition.

EXPERIMENT:

Practice without a Sports Postgame checklist for a week.
Practice with a Sports Postgame checklist for a week.

How do you feel about your competition readiness with a checklist?

How did you feel without a checklist?

Did any questions emerge?

Did you notice anything else?

Did you discover anything that needs to be added to your Sports Skill Practice checklist?

ADVANCED MOVES:

Take what you learn from each competition and revise your Sports Skill Practice checklist.

Buddy up—work with a teammate to create lists, and have your teammate ask you the questions you want to review, then switch.

Activity Checklist

THE JOB IT DOES:

It reduces "Crap! I forgot my [fill in the blank]." moments.

It helps you leave home with all the equipment you need to be successful in your activity.

What to do:

Draft a checklist of items you need for your activity. Remember to include items that need signatures (e.g., permission slips).

EXPERIMENT:

Leave home without an Activity checklist for a week.

Leave home with an Activity checklist for a week.

NOTICE:

How do you feel about your readiness for your activity with a checklist?

How did you feel without a checklist?

Did you feel a "win!"?

Did you notice anything else?

Activity Skill Practice Checklist

THE JOB IT DOES:

It increases the accumulation of experience in skills that will help you master your chosen activity.

WHAT TO DO:

Draft a checklist of the important activities you need to practice to increase your skill for your activity.

EXPERIMENT:

Practice without an Activity Skill Practice checklist for a week.

Practice with an Activity Skill Practice checklist for a week.

NOTICE:

How do you feel about your skill development for your activity with a checklist?

How did you feel without a checklist?

Did you feel a "win!"?

Did you notice anything else?

Did any questions emerge?

Activity Pre-Event Checklist

THE JOB IT DOES:

It increases the ready state for your chosen activity.

WHAT TO DO:

Draft a checklist of the important reminders and activities you need to review or do to help get you optimally ready for your event.

EXPERIMENT:

Practice without an Activity Pre-Event checklist for a week.
Practice with an Activity Pre-Event checklist for a week.

NOTICE:

How do you feel about your event readiness with a checklist?
How did you feel without a checklist?
Did you feel a "win!"?
Did you notice anything else?
Did any questions emerge?

Activity Post-Activity Checklist

THE JOB IT DOES:

It increases your learning capacity for your chosen activity.

WHAT TO DO:

Draft a checklist of the important reminders, questions, and activities you want to review after you complete an event.

EXPERIMENT:

Practice without an Activity Post-Event checklist for a week.
Practice with an Activity Post-Event checklist for a week.

NOTICE:

How do you feel about your competition readiness with a checklist?
How did you feel without a checklist?
Did any questions emerge?
Did you notice anything else?
Did you discover anything that needs to be added to your Activity Skill Practice checklist?

Packing Checklist

THE JOB IT DOES:

It reduces "Crap! I forgot my [fill in the blank]." moments.
It helps you pack with less time and less effort.

WHAT TO DO:

Draft a checklist of things you need to pack for a trip or an overnight stay.

EXPERIMENT:

Prepare for a trip without a packing checklist.
Prepare for a trip with a packing checklist.

NOTICE:

How do you feel while packing?
Did you feel a "win!"?
Did you forget anything? If yes, add it to the checklist.

What I Need to Bring to College Checklist

THE JOB IT DOES:

It reduces "Crap! I forgot my [fill in the blank]." moments.
It helps you pack with less time and less effort.
It helps you pack with an eye toward the space limitations of your college living space.

WHAT TO DO:

Draft a checklist of things you need to bring to college.

EXPERIMENT:

Prepare for college without a packing checklist.
Prepare for college with a packing checklist.

NOTICE:

How do you feel while packing?
Did you feel a "win!"?
Did you forget anything? If yes, add it to the checklist.

Starting a New Semester Checklist

THE JOB IT DOES:

It helps you successfully engage with a new semester.
It helps you register for courses on time.

WHAT TO DO:

Draft a checklist of things you need to do to start a semester.

EXPERIMENT:

Start a semester without a checklist (or notice others'!).
Start a semester with a checklist (or notice others'!).

NOTICE:

How do you feel while signing up for the next semester?
Did you feel a "win!"?
Did you forget anything? If yes, add it to the checklist.
Did you learn anything from last semester that can help you with future semesters? If yes, add it to the checklist.

Back Up Your Phone and/or Computer Checklist

THE JOB IT DOES:

It allows you to recover from hardware failure, stress-free.

WHAT TO DO:

Draft a checklist of things you need to back up on a regular basis.

EXPERIMENT:

Pretend you lost your device. What would you do? What information would be lost?
Use that simulated experience to draft a checklist of items you need to include as part
of your backup plan.

NOTICE:

How do you feel knowing your data is backed up?
Did you feel a "win!"?
Did you forget anything? If yes, add it to the checklist.

LISTS

Lists are how I parse and manage the world.   —ADAM SAVAGE

List of Songs to Purchase

THE JOB IT DOES:

It creates a bucket that allows you to track songs that you might want to purchase in the
future.

WHAT TO DO:

Create a Songs to Get list in your list system.
When a song catches your attention, add it to your list.

Ask your friends and family about their favorite songs.
Add to your list any songs that sound interesting to you.

NOTICE:

What did you capture?
How quickly can you add things to the list?
Where are you storing this list?
How quickly can you pull up the list when you need it for review, reflection, and inspiration?
How does it feel to have a list of songs to purchase?

List of Gift Ideas for Family and Friends

THE JOB IT DOES:

It creates a bucket that allows you to track gifts you might want to get for friends and family.

WHAT TO DO:

When you see something or get a clue from a person that might make a good gift, capture the idea on this list. You're not committing to it. You are simply creating a list of gift-giving options to consider in the future.

EXPERIMENT:

Casually ask your friends and family about the favorite gifts that they've received.
Add any ideas or inspirations to your Gift Ideas list.

How quickly can you add things to the list?
Where are you storing this list?
How quickly can you pull up the list when you need it?
How does it feel to have a list of gift ideas?

List of Quotes

THE JOB IT DOES:

It creates a place to capture quotes that you find interesting or inspiring.

WHAT TO DO:

When you read or hear a quote that you find inspiring or interesting, capture it on this list.

EXPERIMENT:

Over the next week, see how many interesting quotes or song lyrics capture your attention.
Add any quotes to this list.
Review your list at the end of the week.

NOTICE:

What did you capture?
How quickly can you add things to the list?
Where are you storing this list?
How quickly can you pull up the list when you need it for review, reflection, and inspiration?

List of Books to Read

THE JOB IT DOES:

It creates a place to capture books that you might want to read in the future.

WHAT TO DO:

When you hear about a book that sounds interesting to you, capture it on this list.

EXPERIMENT:

Over the next week, ask your friends and family about their favorite books.
Add any books to this list that sound interesting to you.
Review your list at the end of the week.

NOTICE:

What did you capture?
How quickly can you add things to the list?
Where are you storing this list?
How quickly can you pull up the list when you need it for review, reflection, and inspiration?

List of Movies/Shows to Watch

THE JOB IT DOES:

It creates a place to capture movies and shows that you might want to watch in the future.

WHAT TO DO:

When you hear about a movie or a show that sounds interesting to you, capture it on this list.

EXPERIMENT:

Over the next week, ask your friends and family about their favorite movies or shows. Add any movies or shows to this list that sound interesting to you.
Review your list at the end of the week.

NOTICE:

What did you capture?
How quickly can you add things to the list?
Where are you storing this list?
How quickly can you pull up the list when you need it for review, reflection, and inspiration?

List of Video Games to Play

THE JOB IT DOES:

It creates a place to capture games that you might want to play in the future or tips you might want to try to advance your level.

WHAT TO DO:

When you hear about a game or tip that sounds interesting, capture it on this list.

EXPERIMENT:

Over the next week, ask your friends about their games.

Add any games or tips to this list that sound interesting to you.

Review your list at the end of the week.

NOTICE:

What did you capture?

Did your gaming improve?

How quickly can you add things to the list?

Where are you storing this list?

How quickly can you pull up the list when you need it for review, reflection, and inspiration?

List of Questions

THE JOB IT DOES:

It creates a place to capture questions that you find interesting or inspiring. The interesting thing about questions is that they create space for answers.

WHAT TO DO:

When you receive or hear a question that you find inspiring or interesting, capture it on this list.

EXPERIMENT:

Over the next week, see how many interesting questions you can capture.

Add any questions to this list.

Review your list at the end of the week.

NOTICE:

What did you capture?

Did you capture different types of questions?

Do some questions focus your attention differently from others?

How quickly can you add things to the list?

Where are you storing this list?

How quickly can you pull up the list when you need it for review, reflection, and inspiration?

List of Things to Do Next Time I Am in _____

THE JOB IT DOES:

It helps you remember things you'd like to do next time you are in a certain location.

WHAT TO DO:

When you visit a location (e.g., a city or vacation spot) capture things you'd love to do the next time you are there.

EXPERIMENT:

Think back to a location you recently visited where you had a lot of fun.

Next time you are there, is there anything you'd like to do or see? If yes, add it to this list.

NOTICE:

What did you capture?

How quickly can you add things to the list?

Where are you storing this list?

How quickly can you pull up the list when you need it for review, reflection, and inspiration?

List of Birthdays, Anniversaries, and Other Special Dates

THE JOB IT DOES:

It helps you keep track of birthdays and anniversaries that are important to you.

WHAT TO DO:

Create a simple list by month.

Add entries by date under the appropriate month (e.g., Jan-12—Dad's birthday; Mar-3—Anna's birthday; Oct-23—Mom & Dad's anniversary; Nov-14—My birthday!!).

Look at the list at least once a month.

EXPERIMENT:

Add your family's and friends' birthdays and anniversary dates to the list.

NOTICE:

How does it feel to have a simple list of birthdays and anniversary dates?

How quickly can you add things to the list?

Where are you storing this list?

How quickly can you pull up the list when you need it?

Glossary

Amygdala: A part of your brain's front line of defense. This is the fight-or-flight portion of the brain. If the amygdala senses danger or a threat, it will alert your body.

Bucket: A holding bin, either physical or digital, for incoming items still to be processed.

Calendar: Used to track three types of information: (1) Time-specific actions, (2) Day-specific actions, (3) Day-specific reference items. The calendar is the first place to look each day to see the actions you committed to do.

Capture: To gather—and at times generate—items and ideas identified as potentially meaningful, about which one has any attention or interest in possibly deciding or doing something.

Checklist: A personalized list, developed over time, to assist with a specific activity.

Clear: The state of having corralled into buckets physical stuff, digital stuff, and the subtler mental stuff that may be on your mind.

Clarify: To determine the exact meaning of something that emerged from the capture step.

Control: Stability and autonomy within your current reality and circumstances.

Cortland: A wise owl used to personify the prefrontal cortex.

Current: The state of having all lists ("maps") complete and accurate.

Creative: Being creative and taking risks or someday/maybe items. The freedom to be creative comes from being clear and current.

Daily review: A review to help you understand what you need to do today.

Distraction: A pitfall that describes anything that steals your focus away from what you want to focus on.

Engage: To clearly, fully, and confidently do what you know you should be doing in the moment.

GTD: An acronym for Getting Things Done.

Levels of Focus: A model to help you store and retrieve maps and information from different levels of perspective.

Map check: To look back at your calendar, next action list, and/or projects list.

Mind sweep: An activity that involves capturing anything and everything that is on your mind or has your attention.

Myggy: A monkey used to personify the amygdala.

Next action: The next physical, visible activity that progresses something toward completion. This is what "doing" looks like.

Next action list: A complete list of actions that don't need to happen at a specific time or at a specific location.

Open loop: Anything considered unfinished, which, if inappropriately managed, consistently engages one's mind inefficiently.

Organize: To physically, visually, or digitally sort and place items of similar meaning into discrete categories and locations.

Overload: A pitfall that describes the feeling of a large amount of things coming at you in a way that is all just too much, too fast, and too frequent.

Perspective: Your ability to look ahead, to see where you are going and why.

Pitfall: Anything that happens naturally but can lead to problems. The two main pitfalls are overload and distraction.

Planning map: A model that provides a practical recipe for clarifying, planning, and moving anything forward.

Prefrontal cortex: The part of the brain whose function is analytical thought and decision-making. This is the part of the brain that solves problems and synthesizes and makes meaning from all that you see and all that you do.

Project: Any outcome that is going to take more than one action or session to complete.

Projects list: A list that helps keep you on course and contains all the outcomes, or what "done" looks like, on anything you have committed to completing that requires more than one action step.

Ready state: When you're in control of your attention, you are able to relax and apply the appropriate energy and focus to whatever it is that you are doing.

REDS: An acronym that describes Reference, Equipment, Decoration, and Supplies.

Reference: Nonactionable material that needs to be kept but doesn't require any action.

Reflect: To review and update the contents of your maps to bring them up-to-date with your current reality so you can make informed and effective choices.

Someday/Maybe: Anything that you may want to take action on later but doesn't require any action now.

Someday/Maybe list: A list of things you *might* want to do when the opportunity presents itself.

Stuff: Anything that shows up in our world—physically, digitally, mentally, emotionally—that still requires some decision or action and has yet to be determined and isn't yet organized.

Stuff hunt: An activity that involves intentionally scanning your physical or digital environment for anything that isn't REDS and might need your attention.

Surfboard effect: The natural on/off cycle of getting knocked out of the ready state and the ability to get back to it.

Trash: Any nonactionable item that is unneeded and unwanted.

Trigger list: A list that helps trigger thinking during a mind sweep activity.

Two-minute rule: If you can complete an action in less than two minutes, just do it!

Weekly review: A review to help you maintain your ready state by clearing your head, keeping your system current, and stoking your creative energy. It has three parts: Get Clear, Get Current, and Get Creative.

Workstation: Any location where you have access to everything you would need to effectively engage in steps 1 to 3.

Sources

1 http://www.apa.org/news/press/releases/stress/2013/stress-report.pdf
3 https://www.ncbi.nlm.nih.gov/pmc/articles/PMC2864034/

VISUAL SUMMARY

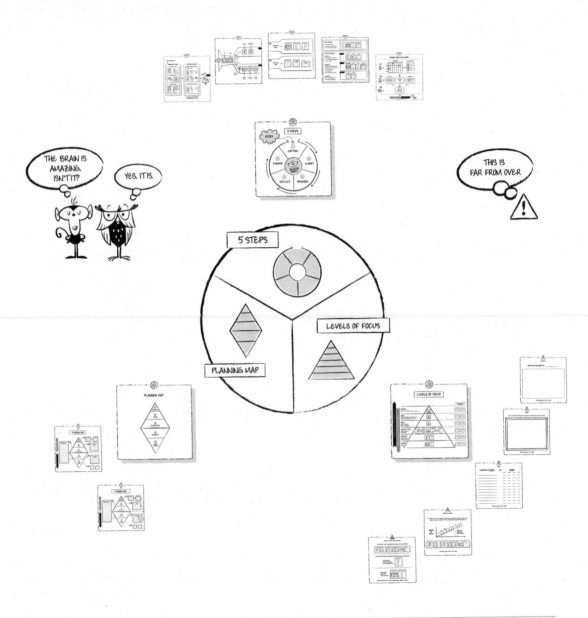

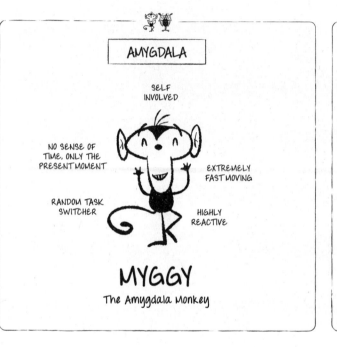

AMYGDALA

SELF INVOLVED

NO SENSE OF TIME, ONLY THE PRESENT MOMENT

EXTREMELY FAST MOVING

RANDOM TASK SWITCHER

HIGHLY REACTIVE

MYGGY

The Amygdala Monkey

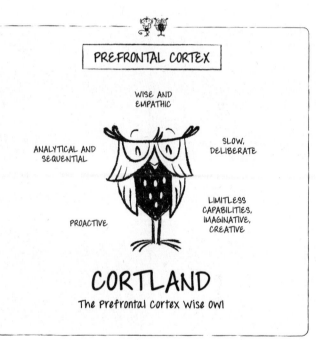

PREFRONTAL CORTEX

WISE AND EMPATHIC

ANALYTICAL AND SEQUENTIAL

SLOW, DELIBERATE

PROACTIVE

LIMITLESS CAPABILITIES, IMAGINATIVE, CREATIVE

CORTLAND

The Prefrontal Cortex Wise Owl

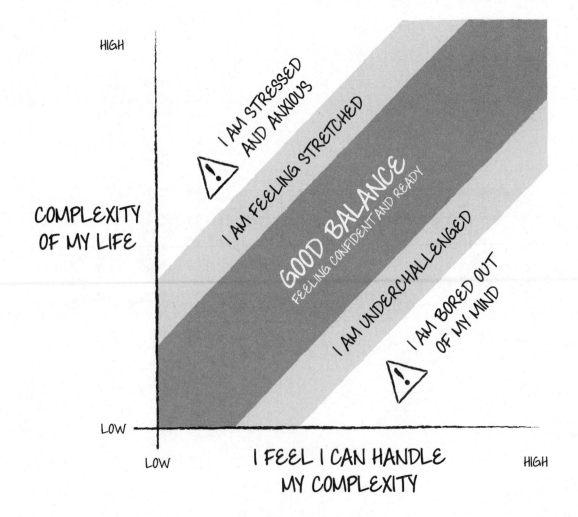

HIGH

COMPLEXITY
OF MY LIFE

I AM STRESSED
AND ANXIOUS

I AM FEELING STRETCHED

GOOD BALANCE
FEELING CONFIDENT AND READY

I AM UNDERCHALLENGED

I AM BORED OUT
OF MY MIND

LOW

LOW   HIGH

I FEEL I CAN HANDLE
MY COMPLEXITY

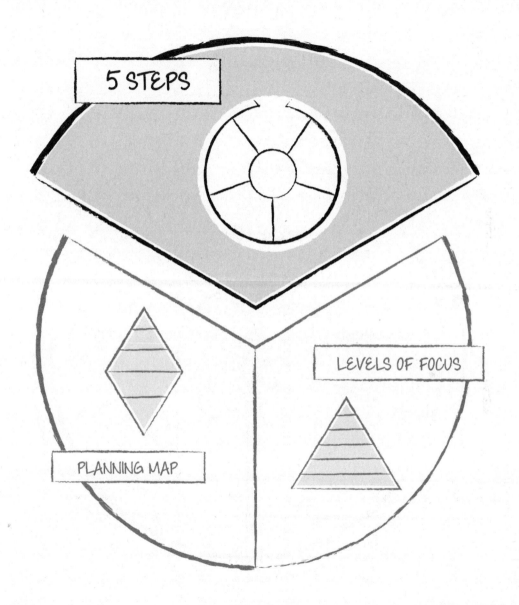

5 STEPS

PLANNING MAP

LEVELS OF FOCUS

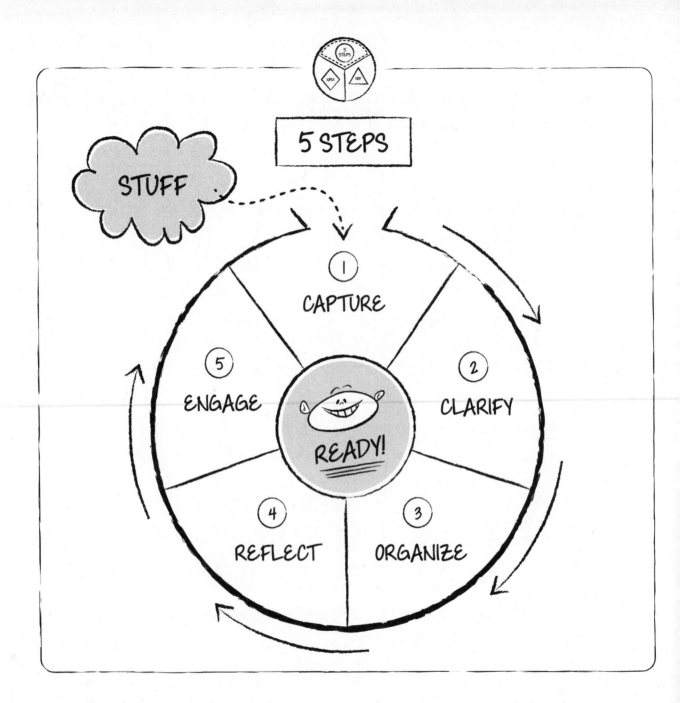

CAPTURE
①

"Life's Random Inputs"

SOURCES OF STUFF

PHYSICAL STUFF

- ☐ Home ☐ _____
- ☐ School ☐ _____
- ☐ Sports ☐ _____
- ☐ Activities ☐ _____

MENTAL STUFF

STUFF STUFF STUFF

MINDSWEEP

DIGITAL STUFF

- ☐ Messaging ☐ School Website
- ☐ Email ☐ Class Website
- ☐ Twitter ☐ Sports Website
- ☐ Facebook ☐ Activity Website
- ☐ Youtube ☐ _____
- ☐ _____ ☐ _____
- ☐ _____ ☐ _____

CAPTURE READY?

CAPTURE TOOLS IN PLACE?

PHYSICAL TOOLS

Y N
☐ ☐ Paper & Pen
☐ ☐ Note Pads
☐ ☐ _____
☐ ☐ _____

DIGITAL TOOLS

☐ ☐ Phone App
☐ ☐ Computer App
☐ ☐ _____

"IN" BUCKETS IN PLACE?

Y N
☐ ☐ Home ☐
☐ ☐ School ☐
☐ ☐ In Transit ☐
☐ ☐ _____
☐ ☐ _____

+

=

CAPTURED!

NEXT,
CLARIFY

"IN"

"Your mind is for having ideas
not holding them." – DAVID ALLEN

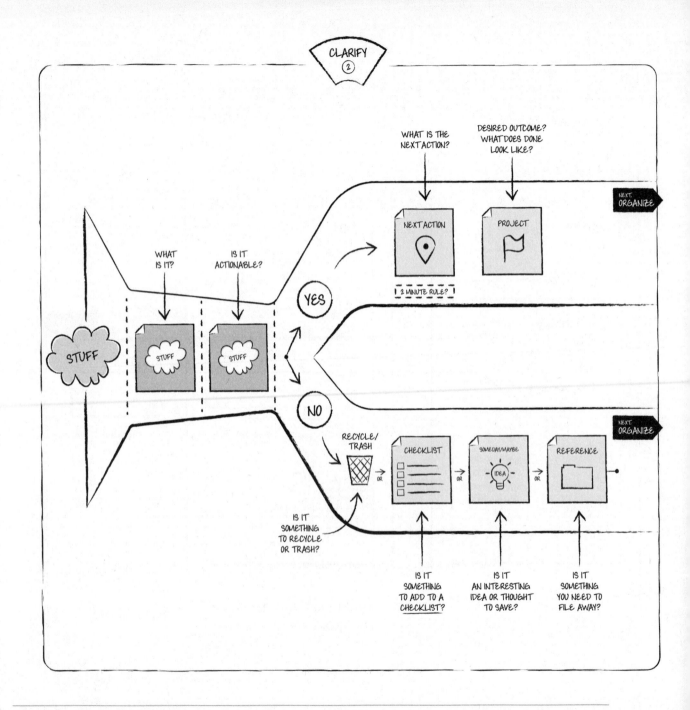

CLARIFY
(2)

STUFF

WHAT
IS IT?

IS IT
ACTIONABLE?

STUFF

STUFF

YES

NO

WHAT IS THE
NEXT ACTION?

DESIRED OUTCOME?
WHAT DOES DONE
LOOK LIKE?

NEXT ACTION

PROJECT

2 MINUTE RULE?

NEXT.
ORGANIZE

RECYCLE/
TRASH

OR

CHECKLIST

OR

SOMEDAY/MAYBE
IDEA

OR

REFERENCE

NEXT.
ORGANIZE

IS IT
SOMETHING
TO RECYCLE
OR TRASH?

IS IT
SOMETHING
TO ADD TO A
CHECKLIST?

IS IT
AN INTERESTING
IDEA OR THOUGHT
TO SAVE?

IS IT
SOMETHING
YOU NEED TO
FILE AWAY?

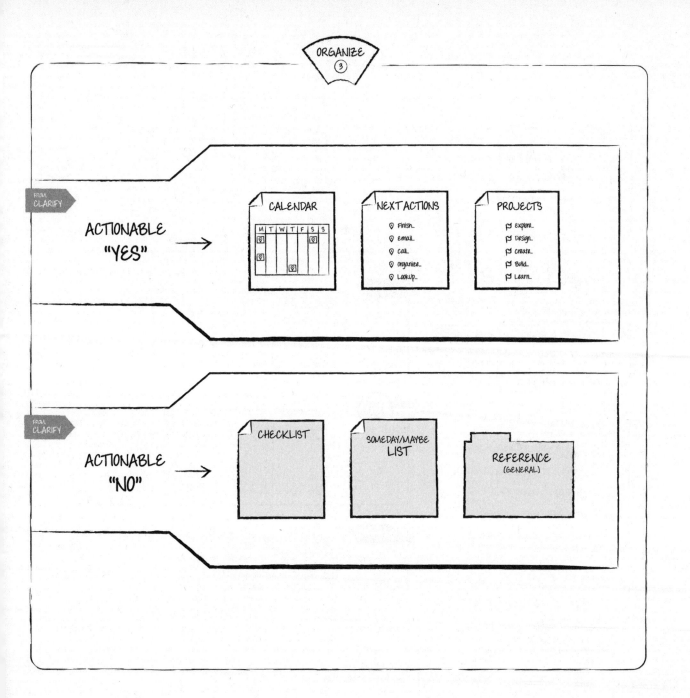

ORGANIZE
3

FROM
CLARIFY

ACTIONABLE
"YES"

CALENDAR

NEXT ACTIONS
- Finish...
- Email...
- Call...
- Organize...
- Lookup...

PROJECTS
- Explore...
- Design...
- Create...
- Build...
- Learn...

FROM
CLARIFY

ACTIONABLE
"NO"

CHECKLIST

SOMEDAY/MAYBE
LIST

REFERENCE
(GENERAL)

REFLECT
(4)

DAILY REVIEW

1. CHECK YOUR CALENDAR
2. CHECK YOUR NEXT ACTION LIST
3. CHECK RELEVANT CHECKLISTS

Check in Morning
↕
Check at Night

WEEKLY REVIEW

GET CLEAR

1. Collect loose papers and materials.
2. Do a mindsweep to empty your head.
3. Get "in" to empty.

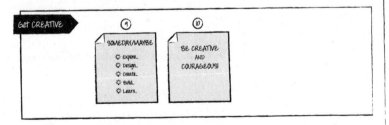

GET CURRENT

4. Review previous calendar entries.
5. Review upcoming calendar entries.
6. Review next action list.
7. Review project list.
8. Review any relevant checklists.

GET CREATIVE

9. Review someday/maybe list.
10. Be creative and courageous!

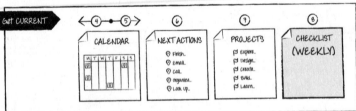

ENGAGE
⑤

Using your maps as your guides...

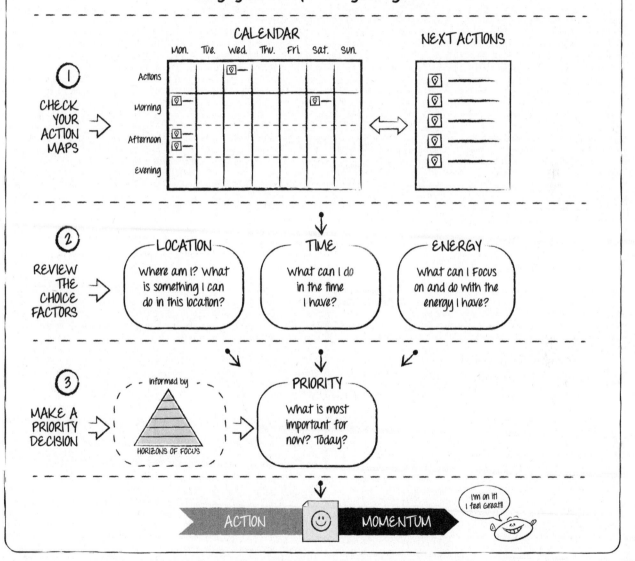

CALENDAR
NEXT ACTIONS

Mon. Tue. Wed. Thu. Fri. Sat. Sun.

Actions
Morning
Afternoon
Evening

① CHECK YOUR ACTION MAPS

② REVIEW THE CHOICE FACTORS

LOCATION
Where am I? What is something I can do in this location?

TIME
What can I do in the time I have?

ENERGY
What can I focus on and do with the energy I have?

③ MAKE A PRIORITY DECISION

Informed by
HORIZONS OF FOCUS

PRIORITY
What is most important for now? Today?

ACTION ☺ MOMENTUM

I'm on it! I feel great!!

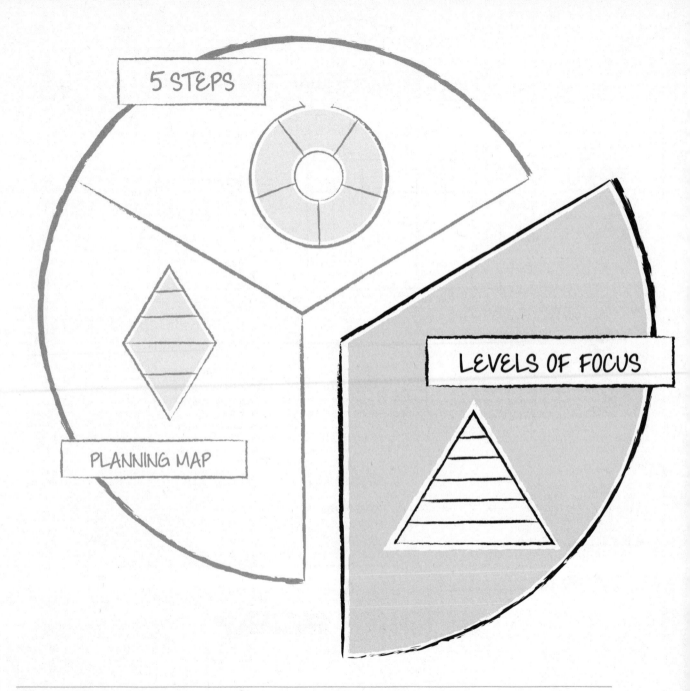

5 STEPS

PLANNING MAP

LEVELS OF FOCUS

LEVELS OF FOCUS

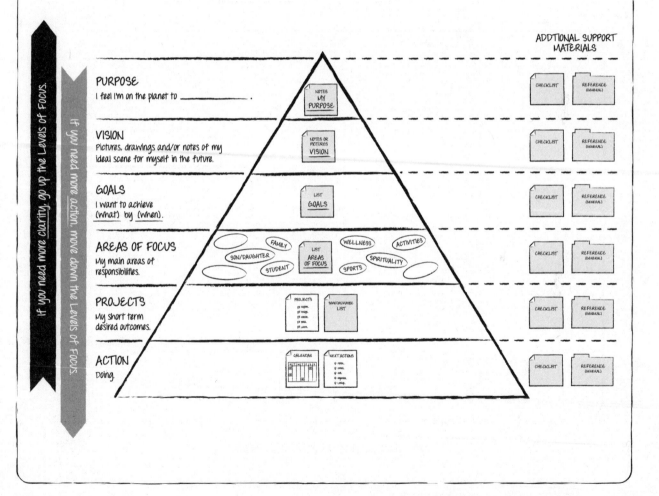

ADDTIONAL SUPPORT MATERIALS

If you need more clarity, go up the Levels of Focus.

If you need more action, move down the Levels of Focus.

PURPOSE
I feel I'm on the planet to _____ .

NOTES MY PURPOSE

CHECKLIST   REFERENCE (GENERAL)

VISION
Pictures, drawings and/or notes of my ideal scene for myself in the future.

NOTES OR PICTURES VISION

CHECKLIST   REFERENCE (GENERAL)

GOALS
I want to achieve (what) by (when).

LIST GOALS

CHECKLIST   REFERENCE (GENERAL)

AREAS OF FOCUS
My main areas of responsibilities.

SON/DAUGHTER   FAMILY   STUDENT   LIST AREAS OF FOCUS   WELLNESS   SPORTS   SPIRITUALITY   ACTIVITIES

CHECKLIST   REFERENCE (GENERAL)

PROJECTS
My short term desired outcomes.

PROJECTS   SOMEDAY/MAYBE LIST

CHECKLIST   REFERENCE (GENERAL)

ACTION
Doing.

CALENDAR   NEXT ACTIONS

CHECKLIST   REFERENCE (GENERAL)

PURPOSE

I feel I'm on the planet to _____ .

(File away in your PURPOSE folder.)

VISION

Here's a vivid picture, drawing, and/or description of what my future will look and feel like.

(File away in your VISION folder.)

GOALS

I would like to (what)   by   (when)

	1 month	1 semester	1 year	1+ years

(File away in your GOALS folder.)

AREAS OF FOCUS

Over time AREAS OF FOCUS transfer from adults in your life (parents, teachers, coaches) to you.
Keeping an eye on your AREAS OF FOCUS will help you handle _any_ transitions in your life.

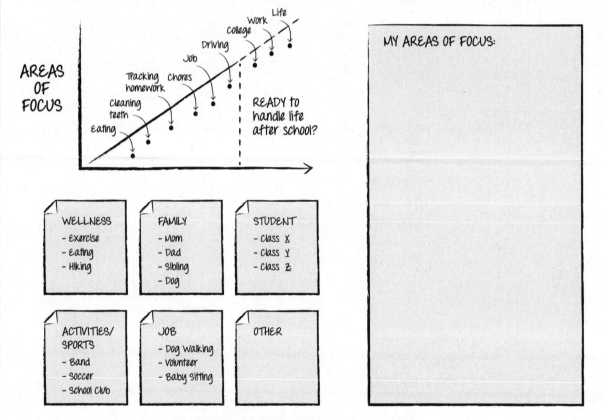

MY AREAS OF FOCUS:

AREAS OF FOCUS

Eating
Cleaning teeth
Tracking homework
Chores
Job
Driving
College
Work
Life

READY to handle life after school?

WELLNESS
- Exercise
- Eating
- Hiking

FAMILY
- Mom
- Dad
- Sibling
- Dog

STUDENT
- Class X
- Class Y
- Class Z

ACTIVITIES/ SPORTS
- Band
- Soccer
- School Club

JOB
- Dog Walking
- Volunteer
- Baby Sitting

OTHER

(File away in your AREAS OF FOCUS folder.)

PROJECTS AND NEXT ACTIONS

Your AREAS OF FOCUS, and higher horizons, hold your focus and direction.

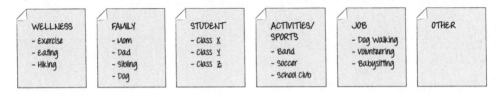

WELLNESS
- Exercise
- Eating
- Hiking

FAMILY
- Mom
- Dad
- Sibling
- Dog

STUDENT
- Class X
- Class Y
- Class Z

ACTIVITIES/ SPORTS
- Band
- Soccer
- School Club

JOB
- Dog Walking
- Volunteering
- Babysitting

OTHER

Your Projects List holds your outcomes that will take more than one next action.

"Projects help us
define the finish line,
what "DONE" looks like."

PROJECTS
- ☐ Explore
- ☐ Design
- ☐ Create
- ☐ Build
- ☐ Learn

"Actions help us
define what
"DOING" looks like."

CALENDAR

M	T	W	T	F	S	S

NEXT ACTIONS
- ⊙ Finish
- ⊙ Email
- ⊙ Call
- ⊙ Organize
- ⊙ Lookup

(File away in PROJECTS & ACTIONS in your planner, agenda, or folders.)

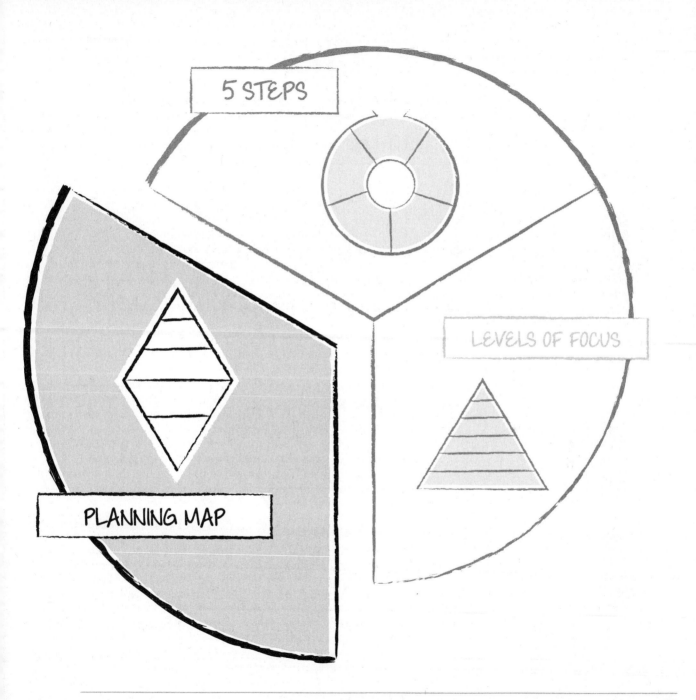

5 STEPS

LEVELS OF FOCUS

PLANNING MAP

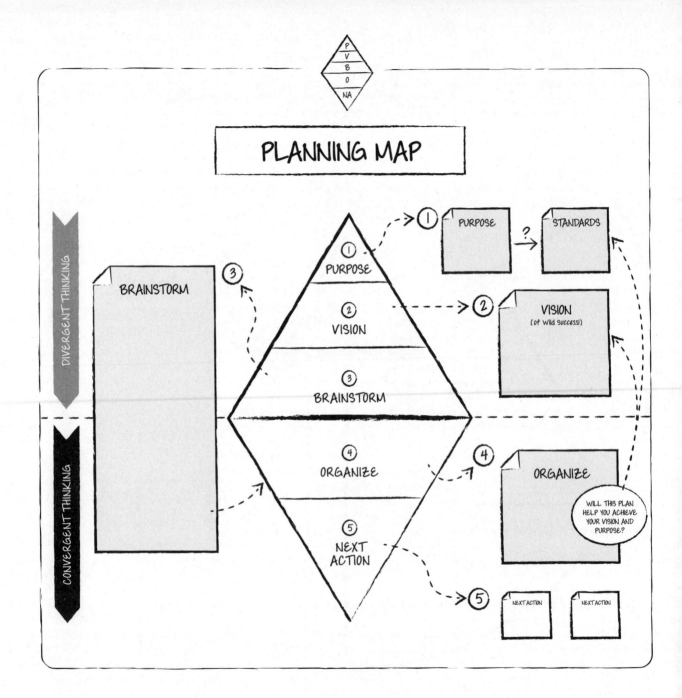

Index

Note: Page numbers in *italics* refer to illustrations.